A HEBREW
READER
for RUTH

DONALD R. VANCE

HENDRICKSON
PUBLISHERS

A Hebrew Reader for Ruth

Printed in the United States of America

Second printing — September 2007

ISBN 978-1-56563-740-5
Hebrew Scripture quotations are from *Biblia Hebraica Leningradensia,* edited by Aron Dotan, copyright © 2001 Hendrickson Publishers, Peabody, Massachusetts, and are used by permission.

Library of Congress Cataloging-in-Publication Data

Bible. O.T. Ruth. Hebrew. 2003.
  A Hebrew reader for Ruth / [commentary & translation] by Donald R. Vance.
      p. cm.
    ISBN 1-56563-740-2 (pbk : alk. paper)
      1. Bible. O.T. Ruth—Textbooks. 2. Hebrew language—Parsing—Textbooks.
I. Vance, Donald R. II. Bible. O.T. Ruth. English. 2003. III. Title.

BS1315.52 .V35 2003
222'.35044—dc21   2002038884

CONTENTS

PREFACE

Anyone who has taught Classical Hebrew for any length of time knows the importance, and the difficulty, of helping students make the transition from completing exercises in an introductory grammar to reading the biblical text on their own. Training students to use the reference grammars so that their learning of Hebrew can continue independently is particularly difficult. After all, what use is knowing the verbal paradigms if the student cannot read a text once they leave the class? It is with this in mind that *A Hebrew Reader for Ruth* was created.

Description

A Hebrew Reader for Ruth presents the complete Hebrew text of the book of Ruth, utilizing the *Biblia Hebraica Leningradensia*. Though text-critical issues are rarely addressed, the Kethib-Qere variants are treated in full.

Beneath the Hebrew text I give my own translation of each verse. Since it is assumed that users of this work will consult other English translations, my translation is intended to illustrate the grammatical peculiarities of the individual verse, and not to provide a smooth rendering of the book as a whole. It serves as a tool to enable the student to understand better the Hebrew. Once students understand the Hebrew, they can evaluate the other translations for themselves.

Following the English translation, each word of the Hebrew text is fully parsed. In addition, wherever one of the standard grammars (see the bibliography) discusses a word or verse, the discussion—either in full quotation or in summary—is included at the appropriate place. These discussions include questions of morphology, lexicography, and syntax. Students are expected to refer to these grammars, and by doing so they will gain competence in their use. Further, unfamiliar but common (others not so common) terms in the study of Hebrew grammar, such as "*nomen rectum,*" "*paragogic nun,*" "optative," "indicative," and the like, will be defined in them. The user of the *Hebrew Reader* should note that, as a rule, only when one of the grammars specifically cites the book of Ruth is the discussion included and all are included. In addition, some of the reference grammars, particularly the German ones, often give long lists of examples of or exceptions to the rules that they are discussing. Several of the references to verses in Ruth fall into this category, and there really is no significant information given by the grammar. For the sake of completeness, these are briefly noted in the *Hebrew Reader* as follows: "On the form, see Berg 2 §5a," or "On the present significance of the perfect here, see Berg 2 §6g," or something similar.

Uses for the Hebrew Reader

The genesis of the *Hebrew Reader* was in my personal study. I decided that I was going to learn Biblical Hebrew thoroughly, and I began creating Hebrew readers for various passages and books of the Hebrew Bible. This evolved into a resource for the classroom, which has proven to be quite successful. The *Hebrew Reader* has proven useful for individual personal study and for classroom use.

For classroom use, the book of Ruth makes an excellent first text for students of Classical Hebrew for several reasons. First, from a grammatical perspective, the book uses for the most part standard morphology, syntax, and vocabulary. Ruth also has an abundance of feminine verbal forms, which reinforces the entire paradigm for the beginning student. Second, Ruth is a well-crafted story, whose character and plot development keep students interested. In a fairly short composition, Ruth introduces students to many of the techniques of biblical Hebrew narrative. Finally, Ruth is a manageable length, which realistically allows for its complete reading in a semester, with plenty of remaining time for detailed discussion of grammatical and interpretive issues.

To facilitate use—whether in the classroom or for personal study—students can fill in the workbook sheets (available at www.hendrickson.com/academic/). By parsing each form and translating each verse, they will reinforce the more common vocabulary and grammatical forms, and they will acquire the discipline of making the translation fit the parsing and context, a skill that is essential for truly understanding the Hebrew Bible.

Finally, I would like to thank John Kutsko for believing in the value of this work and for shepherding it through the entire process. I would also like to thank Bob Buller for his careful typesetting and proofreading of the finished work. It is a joy to work with people who know Hebrew as well as these two.

ABBREVIATIONS

1	first person	Hp	Hophal stem
2	second person	hypoth	hypothetical
3	third person	impf	imperfect *or* imperfective
abs	absolute state	impv	imperative mood
acc	accusative *or* accusatival	indep	independent
act	active voice	indic	indicative mood
adj	adjective	inf	infinitive
adv	adverb	interr	interrogative
art	article	juss	jussive mood
c	common gender	K	Kethib variant
card	cardinal number	L	Leningrad Codex B19a
coh	cohortative mood	loc	locative
conj	conjunction *or* conjunctive	m	masculine gender
cons	consecutive (*also called* conversive *or* retentive)	MS(s)	manuscript(s)
		n	noun
cs	construct state	n.	note
D	Piel stem	N	Niphal stem
def	definite	N.B.	*Nota bene* (= "Note well!")
dem	demonstrative	neg	negative
dir	direct	obj	object
disj	disjunctive	ord	ordinal number
DN	deity name	part	particle
Dp	Pual stem	pass	passive voice
du	dual	pers	personal
f	feminine gender	pf	perfect or perfective
G	Qal stem	pl	plural
gen	genitive or genitival	*pl. tan.*	*plurali tantum* (= "only plural," i.e., a word that occurs only in the plural)
gent	gentilic		
GN	geographic name		
H	Hiphil stem	PN	personal name

pref	prefix(ed)		subs	substantive
prep	preposition		sx	suffix
pron	pronoun		tD	Hithpael stem
prox	proximal (i.e., "near")		temp	temporal
ptc	participle		v	verb
Q	Qere variant		w/	with
rel	relative		√	root
s	singular		=	equals, is the same as
s.v.	*sub verbo* (= "under the word," i.e., an entry in the lexicon)		≈	approximates, is roughly the same as
st. pr.	*status pronominalus* (= pronominal suffix form)			

BIBLIOGRAPHY

Citation is made to the lexica by entry (indicated with the abbreviation *s.v.*). The grammars are cited by section number (indicated by §) and paragraph letter (e.g., GKC §127f), except for Seow and Driver, which are cited by page number (e.g., Seow, p. 175), and for *GAHG,* which is cited by volume number (it has three volumes) followed by page number (e.g., GAHG 3:146). Bergsträsser's grammar is in two volumes (reprinted in one book, but with separate pagination for each volume), and the volume number precedes the § symbol (e.g., Berg 2 §8c = volume 2, section 8, paragraph c). Further, he uses roman paragraph letters for paragraphs in the body of the text and italicized paragraph letters for the notes at the bottom of the page (e.g., Berg 2 §*8c* is a note located at the bottom of the page). A paragraph letter with an asterisk (evidently indicating an inserted paragraph) immediately follows the same paragraph letter without the asterisk; that is, Berg 2 §8c* is found immediately after Berg 2 §8c.

BDB   Brown, Francis, S. R. Driver, Charles A. Briggs. *A Hebrew and English Lexicon of the Old Testament*. Oxford: Oxford University Press, 1907. Repr., Peabody, Mass.: Hendrickson, 1996. Corrected ed., Oxford: Oxford University Press, 1953.

Berg   Bergsträsser, Gotthelf. *Hebräische Grammatik: mit Benutzung der von E. Kautzsch bearbeiteten 28. Auflage von Wilhelm Gesenius' hebräischer Grammatik*. 2 vols. Leipzig: Hinrichs, 1918. Repr. 2 vols. in 1, Hildesheim: Olms, 1962.

BHL   Dotan, Aron, ed. *Biblia Hebraica Leningradensia: Prepared according to the Vocalization, Accents, and Masora of Aaron ben Moses ben Asher in the Leningrad Codex*. Peabody, Mass.: Hendrickson, 2001.

BHRG   van der Merwe, Christo H. J., Jackie A. Naudé, and Jan H. Kroeze. *A Biblical Hebrew Reference Grammar*. Biblical Languages: Hebrew 3. Edited by Stanley E. Porter and Richard S. Hess. Sheffield: Sheffield Academic Press, 1999.

BHS   Elliger, Karl, and Wilhelm Rudolph, eds. *Biblia Hebraica Stuttgartensia*. 5th printing. Stutt-gart: Deutsche Bibelgesellschaft, 1997.

BL   Bauer, Hans, and Pontus Leander. *Historische Grammatik der Hebräischen Sprache des Alten Testamentes*. Halle: Niemeyer: 1918–1922. Repr., Hildesheim: Olms, 1965.

Brock   Brockelmann, Carl. *Hebräische Syntax*. Neukirchen: Neukirchener Verlag, 1956.

DCH   Clines, David J. A., ed. *The Dictionary of Classical Hebrew.* Sheffield, England: Sheffield Academic Press, 1993–.

Driver   Driver, Samuel Rolles. *A Treatise on the Use of the Tenses in Hebrew and Some Other Syntactical Questions.* Biblical Resource. 4th ed. (repr. of 3d ed. with new introduction by W. Randall Garr) London: Oxford University Press, 1892. Repr., Grand Rapids, Mich.: Eerdmans; Livonia, Mich.: Dove Booksellers, 1998.

GAHG   Richter, Wolfgang. *Grundlagen einer althebräischen Grammatik.* Arbeiten zu Text und Sprache im alten Testament 8, 10, and 13. Edited by Wolfgang Richter. St. Ottilien: Eos Verlag, 1978–1980.

GKC   Kautzsch, E., ed. *Gesenius' Hebrew Grammar.* Translated by A. E. Cowley. 2d ed. Oxford: Oxford University Press, 1910.

HALOT   Koehler, Ludwig, Walter Baumgartner, and J. J. Stamm. *The Hebrew and Aramaic Lexicon of the Old Testament.* Translated and edited under the supervision of M. E. J. Richardson. 5 vols. Leiden: Brill, 1994–2000.

IBHS   Waltke, Bruce K., and Michael O'Connor. *An Introduction to Biblical Hebrew Syntax.* Winona Lake, Ind.: Eisenbrauns, 1990.

Joüon   Joüon, Paul. *Grammaire de l'hébreu biblique.* 2d ed. Rome: Pontifical Biblical Institute, 1923.

Lambdin   Lambdin, Thomas O. *Introduction to Biblical Hebrew.* New York: Charles Scribner's Sons, 1971.

Seow   Seow, Choon Leong. *A Grammar for Biblical Hebrew.* Revised ed. Nashville: Abingdon, 1995.

Vance   Vance, Donald R. *Introduction to Classical Hebrew.* Boston: Brill, 2005.

Wms   Williams, Ronald James. *Hebrew Syntax: An Outline.* Toronto: University of Toronto Press, 1976.

Yeivin   Yeivin, Israel. *Introduction to the Tiberian Masorah.* Translated and edited by E. J. Revell. Masoretic Studies 5. Missoula, Mont.: Scholars Press, 1980.

RUTH 1:1–22

וַיְהִי בִּימֵי שְׁפֹט הַשֹּׁפְטִים וַיְהִי רָעָב בָּאָרֶץ וַיֵּלֶךְ אִישׁ מִבֵּית לֶחֶם יְהוּדָה לָגוּר **1:1**
בִּשְׂדֵי מוֹאָב הוּא וְאִשְׁתּוֹ וּשְׁנֵי בָנָיו:

1:1   Back in the days when the judges judged, there was a famine in the land, and a man from Bethlehem of Judah went to stay a while in the regions of Moab: he, his wife, and his two sons.

וַיְהִי	v, G, impf, indic, 3, m, s √היה w/ ו cons "and it was"
	On a book beginning with a *wāw* consecutive, see Berg 2 §8a* and GKC §49b n. 1. According to GKC §111f–g, Joüon §118c n. 2, Lambdin §110, *IBHS* §33.2.4b, and Vance §15.5.1, a circumstantial clause (a clause that gives the circumstances under which the main clause takes place) is often introduced by וַיְהִי, and the main clause follows, introduced by the next *wayyqtl* form.
בִּימֵי	n, m, pl, cs יוֹם w/ prep בְּ "in the days of"
שְׁפֹט	v, G, inf, cs √שפט "the judging of"
הַשֹּׁפְטִים	v, G, act, ptc, m, pl, abs √שפט w/ def art "the judges"
	According to *IBHS* §37.1c, the active participle has four functions in Biblical Hebrew, one of which is as a substantive.
וַיְהִי	v, G, impf, indic, 3, m, s √היה w/ ו cons "there was"
	According to *IBHS* §33.2.4b and Vance §15.5.1, a *wayyqtl* form introduces the main clause after a circumstantial clause introduced by וַיְהִי. Thus, this second וַיְהִי is introducing the main clause. However, one could argue that this second וַיְהִי is introducing yet another circumstantial clause and that וַיֵּלֶךְ below is introducing the main clause. This would yield, "Back in the days when the

judges were judging and there was a famine in the land, a man from Bethlehem of Judah went.... "

רָעָב   n, m, s, abs רָעָב √רעב "a famine"

בָּאָרֶץ   n, f, s, abs אֶרֶץ √ארץ "land" w/ prep בְּ and def art "in the land"

וַיֵּלֶךְ   v, G, impf, indic, 3, m, s √הלך w/ ו cons "and he went"

אִישׁ   n, m, s, abs אִישׁ √אנשׁ? "a man"

מִבֵּית לֶחֶם   GN, cs w/ prep מִן "from Bethlehem of"
Geographical names of the form *bêt*-X almost always denote the location of a temple to the god X, such as בֵּית־שֶׁמֶשׁ denoting the temple of Shamshu (the Canaanite sun god). Consequently, בֵּית־לֶחֶם means temple of Laḥmu (a Canaanite god of war; see √לחם in the N stem), not House of Bread or Storehouse of Bread. According to *BHRG* §32.2.4 (and also §39.3 [iv]), "a prepositional phrase can function as an adjectival qualification," and they translate our clause, "a man of Bethlehem in Judah."

יְהוּדָה   GN "Judah"

לָגוּר   v, G, inf, cs √גור w/ prep לְ "to sojourn"

בִּשְׂדֵי   n, m, pl, cs שָׂדֶה √שׂדה w/ prep בְּ "in the fields of"
BL §73l parse this as a singular (presumably because all the other occurrences of this word in Ruth are singular) and list this as a deviant form.

מוֹאָב   GN "Moab"

הוּא   indep pers pron, 3, m, s הוּא "he"
According to Joüon §146c, "When one adds a second subject [here וְאִשְׁתּוֹ וּשְׁנֵי בָנָיו], after a separating word [here מִבֵּית לֶחֶם יְהוּדָה לָגוּר בִּשְׂדֵי מוֹאָב], to a nominal subject [here אִישׁ], a resumptive pronoun [here הוּא] is necessary." So also *IBHS* §16.3.2b–c, which adds that the resumptive pronoun is "not pleonastic or emphatic; it serves merely to represent the referent of the pronoun as the chief actor among other actors." According to *BHRG* §34.1 (iii), "With so-called *split subjects* the word chain that specifies the subject may stand at the *end of a clause.*"

וְאִשְׁתּוֹ   n, f, s, *st. pr.* אִשָּׁה √אנשׁ w/ 3, m, s, gen sx and ו conj "and his wife"

וּשְׁנֵי   card, m, du, cs שְׁנַיִם √שׁנהIII w/ ו conj "and the two of"
According to Brock §84a, in Ruth the numbers precede the thing being counted almost exclusively.

בָּנָיו   n, m, pl, *st. pr.* בֵּן √בנה? w/ 3, m, s, gen sx "his sons"

(βstop)

1:2 וְשֵׁם הָאִישׁ אֱלִימֶ֫לֶךְ וְשֵׁם אִשְׁתּוֹ נָעֳמִי וְשֵׁם שְׁנֵי־בָנָיו ׀ מַחְלוֹן וְכִלְיוֹן אֶפְרָתִים מִבֵּית לֶחֶם יְהוּדָה וַיָּבֹאוּ שְׂדֵי־מוֹאָב וַיִּהְיוּ־שָׁם׃

1:2 Now the man's name was Elimelech, his wife's name was Naomi, and the names of his two sons were Mahlon and Chilion. Ephrathites from Bethlehem of Judah, they came to the regions of Moab and stayed there.

וְשֵׁם	n, m, s, cs שֵׁם w/ ו disj "and the name of"
הָאִישׁ	n, m, s, abs אִישׁ √אנש? w/ def art "the man" *IBHS* §13.5.1d: "Particular reference [by means of the article] may be based on previous mention of the thing or person [see אִישׁ in the preceding verse]; such use is *anaphoric*." To convey this sense, they translate our word "that man." See also Joüon §137f.
אֱלִימֶ֫לֶךְ	PN "Elimelech" Note the *metheg* within the *ḥāṭēp sĕgōl* under the א. A *metheg* generally appears to the left of a vowel; less often it is written to the right, and rarely, as here, it appears in the middle of a *ḥāṭēp* vowel. See Yeivin §314.
וְשֵׁם	n, m, s, cs שֵׁם w/ ו conj "and the name of"
אִשְׁתּוֹ	n, f, s, *st. pr.* אִשָּׁה √אנש w/ 3, m, s, gen sx "his wife"
נָעֳמִי	PN "Naomi" If this name were transliterated strictly, it would be *Noʿŏmî*.
וְשֵׁם	n, m, s, cs שֵׁם w/ ו conj "and the name of" It is not uncommon in Ruth for there not to be number (even gender!) agreement between the parts of a clause, such as this singular subject (שֵׁם) with a compound predicate (מַחְלוֹן וְכִלְיוֹן). We would expect the plural construct שְׁמוֹת. According to Joüon §136l, there is a tendency to use a singular instead of a plural where several individuals have similar things, such as *name* here.
שְׁנֵי־	card, m, du, cs שְׁנַ֫יִם √שנהIII "the two of"
בָנָיו	n, m, pl, *st. pr.* בֵּן √בנה? w/ 3, m, s, gen sx "his sons"
מַחְלוֹן	PN "Mahlon"
וְכִלְיוֹן	PN w/ ו conj "and Chilion" If this name were transliterated strictly, it would be *Kilyôn*.
אֶפְרָתִים	gent adj, m, pl, abs אֶפְרָתִי "Ephrathites," i.e., "those from Ephrathah" On the gentilic form of adjectives, see GKC §86h.

מִבֵּית לֶחֶם	GN, cs w/ prep מִן "from Bethlehem of"
יְהוּדָה	GN "Judah"
וַיָּבֹאוּ	v, G, impf, indic, 3, m, pl √בוא w/ ו cons "and they went to"
שְׂדֵי־	n, m, pl, cs שָׂדֶה √שׂדה "the fields of"
מוֹאָב	GN "Moab"
וַיִּהְיוּ־	v, G, impf, indic, 3, m, pl √היה w/ ו cons "and they were [≈ lived]"
שָׁם	loc adv "there"

1:3 וַיָּמָת אֱלִימֶלֶךְ אִישׁ נָעֳמִי וַתִּשָּׁאֵר הִיא וּשְׁנֵי בָנֶיהָ:

1:3 Elimelech, the husband of Naomi, died, and she was left, as were her two sons.

וַיָּמָת	v, G, impf, indic, 3, m, s √מות w/ ו cons "and he died"
אֱלִימֶלֶךְ	PN "Elimelech"
אִישׁ	n, m, s, cs אִישׁ √אנשׁ? "the husband of" *IBHS* §13.4c: "The *construct relation* usually carries definiteness over from the genitive to the construct: thus, the construct is usually definite if the following genitive is definite as a name…, a pronoun…, a unique appellative…, or because of the article."
נָעֳמִי	PN "Naomi"
וַתִּשָּׁאֵר	v, N, impf, indic, 3, f, s √שׁאר w/ ו cons "and she remained" It is common to encounter number (or gender) disagreement between the parts of a clause in Ruth (here, a plural subject of mixed gender with a feminine singular verb). On the other hand, one may understand וּשְׁנֵי בָנֶיהָ as a parenthetical expression. Berg 2 §16g lists our word here as an exception to the rule that immediately before another accent (such as when the next word is monosyllabic, as here), the *ṣērê* of the N stem should become *sĕgōl*.
הִיא	indep pers pron, 3, f, s הִיא "she" Joüon §146c: "When one adds a second subject to the pronominal subject contained virtually in a verbal form, a resumptive pronoun is necessary." See also *IBHS* §16.3.2b–c.
וּשְׁנֵי	card, m, du, cs שְׁנַיִם √שׁנה III w/ ו conj "and the two of"

בָנֶיהָ   n, m, pl, *st. pr.* בֵּן √בנה? w/ 3, f, s, gen sx "her two sons"

1:4 וַיִּשְׂאוּ לָהֶם נָשִׁים מֹאֲבִיּוֹת שֵׁם הָאַחַת עָרְפָּה וְשֵׁם הַשֵּׁנִית רוּת וַיֵּשְׁבוּ שָׁם כְּעֶשֶׂר שָׁנִים:

1:4   They married Moabite women: the name of the one was Orpah, and the name of the second was Ruth. They lived there about ten years.

וַיִּשְׂאוּ   v, G, impf, indic, 3, m, pl √נשא w/ ו cons "and they lifted up [≈ married]"

לָהֶם   prep לְ w/ 3, m, pl, gen sx "to themselves"

נָשִׁים   n, f, pl, abs אִשָּׁה √אנש "women; wives"
The expression "they lifted up to themselves Moabite women" means "they married Moabite women."

מֹאֲבִיּוֹת   gent adj, f, pl, abs מוֹאֲבִיָּה (m, s מוֹאָבִי) "Moabitesses"

שֵׁם   n, m, s, cs שֵׁם "the name of"

הָאַחַת   card, f, s, abs אֶחָד √אחד w/ def art "the one"

עָרְפָּה   PN "Orpah"

וְשֵׁם   n, m, s, cs שֵׁם w/ ו conj "and the name of"

הַשֵּׁנִית   ord, f, s, abs שֵׁנִית (m = שֵׁנִי) √שנהIII w/ def art "the second"

רוּת   PN "Ruth"

וַיֵּשְׁבוּ   v, G, impf, indic, 3, m, pl √ישב w/ ו cons "and they dwelled"

שָׁם   loc adv "there"

כְּעֶשֶׂר   card, f, s, cs עֶשֶׂר √עשר w/ prep כְּ "about ten [of]"
On the use of כְּ to indicate approximation, see Wms §257, Joüon §133g, and *IBHS* §11.2.9b. The latter state: "There are three facets to the basic use of כְּ. (1) The preposition may denote *agreement in quantity or measure,* as in 'Moses is *as* tall *as* Joshua'.... Related to this is the use of the preposition before *approximations,* as in 'Moses is *about* that tall.'" (Their other uses of כְּ are agreement in kind and correspondence or identity.) According to Brock §109b, this use of כְּ is quite normal before statements of time.

שָׁנִים   n, f, pl, abs שָׁנָה √שנה "years"

1:5 וַיָּמֻ֣תוּ גַם־שְׁנֵיהֶ֖ם מַחְל֣וֹן וְכִלְי֑וֹן וַתִּשָּׁאֵר֙ הָֽאִשָּׁ֔ה מִשְּׁנֵ֥י יְלָדֶ֖יהָ וּמֵאִישָֽׁהּ׃

1:5 Both Mahlon and Chilion also died, and the woman was left without her children and her husband.

וַיָּמֻ֣תוּ	v, G, impf, indic, 3, m, pl √מות w/ ו cons "and they died"
גַם־	adv גַּם √גמם "also"
שְׁנֵיהֶ֖ם	card, m, du, cs שְׁנַ֫יִם √שנהIII w/ 3, m, pl, gen sx "the two of them"
מַחְל֣וֹן	PN "Mahlon"
וְכִלְי֑וֹן	PN w/ ו conj "and Chilion"
וַתִּשָּׁאֵר֙	v, N, impf, indic, 3, f, s √שאר w/ ו cons "and she remained"
	Berg 2 §16g lists our word here as an exception to the tendency of the N imperfect consecutive to have a *sĕgōl* with accent retraction (e.g., וַיִּשָּׁ֫אֶר in Gen 7:23).
הָֽאִשָּׁ֔ה	n, f, s, abs אִשָּׁה √אנש w/ def art "the wife (i.e., Naomi)"
מִשְּׁנֵ֥י	card, m, du, cs שְׁנַ֫יִם √שנהIII w/ prep מִן "from the two of"
	On the separating sense of מִן here, see Brock §111c.
יְלָדֶ֖יהָ	n, m, pl, *st. pr.* יֶ֫לֶד √ילד w/ 3, f, s, gen sx "her children"
וּמֵאִישָֽׁהּ	n, m, s, *st. pr.* אִישׁ √אנש? w/ 3, f, s, gen sx, prep מִן , and ו conj "from her husband"

1:6 וַתָּ֤קָם הִיא֙ וְכַלֹּתֶ֔יהָ וַתָּ֖שָׁב מִשְּׂדֵ֣י מוֹאָ֑ב כִּ֤י שָֽׁמְעָה֙ בִּשְׂדֵ֣ה מוֹאָ֔ב כִּֽי־פָקַ֤ד יְהוָה֙ אֶת־עַמּ֔וֹ לָתֵ֥ת לָהֶ֖ם לָֽחֶם׃

1:6 She and her daughters-in-law arose and headed back from the regions of Moab, for she had heard in the region of Moab that YHWH had attended to his people by giving them food.

וַתָּ֤קָם	v, G, impf, indic, 3, f, s √קום w/ ו cons "and she arose"
	It is not uncommon in Ruth for there not to be number (even gender!) agreement between the parts of a clause, such as this singular verb (וַתָּ֫קָם) with a compound subject (הִיא֙ וְכַלֹּתֶ֫יהָ).
הִיא֙	indep pers pron, 3, f, s הִיא "she"
	Joüon §146c: "When one adds a second subject to the pronominal subject contained virtually in a verbal form, a resumptive pronoun is necessary." See also *IBHS* §16.3.2b–c.

6

וְכַלֹּתֶיהָ   n, f, pl, *st. pr.* כַּלָּה √כלל w/ 3, f, s, gen sx and ו conj "and her daughters-in-law"

וַתָּשָׁב   v, G, impf, indic, 3, f, s √שׁוב w/ ו cons "and she returned"
IBHS §16.3.2c (also §16.3.2b): "The singular verb before a plural coordinate subject is commonplace.... Here the pronoun [הִיא of this verse] is not pleonastic or emphatic; it serves merely to represent the referent of the pronoun as the chief actor among other actors."

מִשְּׂדֵי   n, m, pl, cs שָׂדֶה √שׂדה w/ prep מִן "from the fields of"

מוֹאָב   GN "Moab"

כִּי   conj כִּי "that, for, when"

שָׁמְעָה   v, G, pf, 3, f, s √שׁמע "she heard"

בִּשְׂדֵה   n, m, s, cs שָׂדֶה √שׂדה w/ prep בְּ "in the field of"

מוֹאָב   GN "Moab"

כִּי   conj כִּי "that, for, when"

פָּקַד   v, G, pf, 3, m, s √פקד "he attended to, visited"

יְהוָה   DN "YHWH"
Precisely how the Tetragrammaton (Latin for *the four letters*) was vocalized is the subject of no small debate (see GKC §102m, Joüon 16f 1, and *s.v.* in the lexicons). I have chosen merely to transliterate the four consonants.

אֶת־   sign def dir obj

עַמּוֹ   n, m, s, *st. pr.* עַם √עמם w/ 3, m, s, gen sx "his people"

לָתֵת   v, G, inf, cs √נתן w/ לְ "to give"

לָהֶם   prep לְ w/ 3, m, pl, gen sx "to them"

לָחֶם   n, m, s, pausal form לֶחֶם √לחם "bread"

1:7 וַתֵּצֵא מִן־הַמָּקוֹם אֲשֶׁר הָיְתָה־שָּׁמָּה וּשְׁתֵּי כַלֹּתֶיהָ עִמָּהּ וַתֵּלַכְנָה בַדֶּרֶךְ לָשׁוּב אֶל־אֶרֶץ יְהוּדָה:

1:7 She went out from the place where she had been, her two daughters-in-law with her, and they set out on the way to return to the land of Judah.

וַתֵּצֵא   v, G, impf, indic, 3, f, s √יצא w/ ו cons "and she went out"

מִן־	prep מִן "from"
הַמָּקוֹם	n, m, s, abs קום√ מָקוֹם w/ def art "the place"
אֲשֶׁר	rel pron אשר√ אֲשֶׁר "that"
הָיְתָה	v, G, pf, 3, f, s היה√ "she was"
שָׁמָּה	loc adv שָׁם w/ loc ה "to there"
וּשְׁתֵּי	card, f, cs שָׁנַיִם√שנה III w/ ו conj "and the two of"
כַלֹּתֶיהָ	n, f, pl, *st. pr.* כַּלָּה√ כלל w/ 3, f, s, gen sx "her daughters-in-law"
עִמָּהּ	prep עִם w/ 3, f, s, gen sx "with her"
וַתֵּלַכְנָה	v, G, impf, indic, 3, f, pl הלך√ w/ ו cons "and they went"
בַּדֶּרֶךְ	n, m, s, abs דֶּרֶךְ√ דרך w/ prep בְּ and def art "in the way"
לָשׁוּב	v, G, inf, cs שוב√ w/ prep לְ "to return"
אֶל־	prep אֶל "to"
אֶרֶץ	n, f, s, cs אֶרֶץ√ ארץ "the land of"
יְהוּדָה	GN "Judah"

1:8 וַתֹּאמֶר נָעֳמִי לִשְׁתֵּי כַלֹּתֶיהָ לֵכְנָה שֹּׁבְנָה אִשָּׁה לְבֵית אִמָּהּ יַעֲשֶׂה [יַעַשׂ] יְהוָה עִמָּכֶם חֶסֶד כַּאֲשֶׁר עֲשִׂיתֶם עִם־הַמֵּתִים וְעִמָּדִי:

1:8 Naomi said to her two daughters-in-law, "Go! Each return to the house of her mother! May YHWH show covenant-loyalty with you just as you have shown with the dead and with me."

וַתֹּאמֶר	v, G, impf, indic, 3, f, s אמר√ w/ ו cons "and she said"
נָעֳמִי	PN "Naomi"
לִשְׁתֵּי	ord, f, cs שָׁנַיִם√שנה III w/ prep לְ "to the two of"
כַלֹּתֶיהָ	n, f, pl, *st. pr.* כַּלָּה√ כלל w/ 3, f, s, gen sx "her daughters-in-law"
לֵכְנָה	v, G, impf, impv, 2, f, pl הלך√ "go!" On הלך√ conforming to the pattern of I-י roots, see Berg 2 §26o.
שֹּׁבְנָה	v, G, impf, impv, 2, f, pl שוב√ "return!"

Note the *dagesh forte* in the שׁ, which indicates that לְכֵנָה שֹּׁבְנָה was pronounced as one word, showing the close connection of the two words. On the form, see Berg 2 §28f.

אִשָּׁה	n, f, s, abs אִשָּׁה √אנשׁ "woman [≈ each]"
לְבֵית	n, m, s, cs בַּיִת w/ prep לְ "to the house of"
אִמָּהּ	n, f, s, *st. pr.* אֵם √אמם w/ 3, f, s, gen sx "her mother"
יַעֲשֶׂה	K, v, G, impf, indic, 3, m, s √עשׂה "he will do"
יַעַשׂ	Q, v, G, impf, juss, 3, m, s √עשׂה "may he do" On the force of the jussive as blessing, see Berg 2 §10*b*.
יְהוָה	DN "YHWH"
עִמָּכֶם	prep עִם √עמם w/ 2, m, pl, gen sx "with you" GKC §135o: "Through a weakening in the distinction of gender,... *masculine* suffixes (especially in the plural) are not infrequently used to refer to *feminine* substantives." As has been pointed out earlier, it is not uncommon in Ruth for there not to be gender (and, as we have seen, number) agreement between the parts of a clause; here, a masculine plural pronominal suffix refers to the two women, Ruth and Orpah. See also Brock §124b, Joüon §149b, and Wms §234.
חֶסֶד	n, m, s, abs חֶסֶד √חסד "covenant-loyalty"
כַּאֲשֶׁר	rel pron אֲשֶׁר √אשׁר w/ prep כְּ "just as"
עֲשִׂיתֶם	v, G, pf, 2, m, pl √עשׂה "you did" In addition to GKC §135o, Brock §124b, Joüon §150a, and Wms §234, see also GKC §144a, which states, "Not infrequently ... masculine forms are used in referring to feminines" and lists this word as an example. *IBHS* 6.6c explains, "since there are cases of a masculine plural verb following a feminine plural noun, ... it has been suggested that [such] types of discord reflect an avoidance of feminine plural verbs."
עִם־	prep עִם √עמם "with"
הַמֵּתִים	v, G, act, ptc, m, pl, abs √מות w/ def art "the dead" According to *IBHS* §37.1c, the active participle has four functions in Biblical Hebrew: as a substantive, as an adjective, as a relative (i.e., the participle modifies an antecedent substantive), and as a predicate. In this case the participle is functioning as a substantive.
וְעִמָּדִי	prep עִם √עמם w/ 1, c, s, gen sx and וְ conj "and with me"

1:9 יִתֵּן֩ יְהוָ֨ה לָכֶ֜ם וּמְצֶ֣אןָ מְנוּחָ֗ה אִשָּׁ֖ה בֵּ֣ית אִישָׁ֑הּ וַתִּשַּׁ֣ק לָהֶ֔ן וַתִּשֶּׂ֥אנָה קוֹלָ֖ן וַתִּבְכֶּֽינָה׃

1:9 "May YHWH grant that you find rest, each in the house of her husband!" She kissed them, and they lifted up their voice and wept.

יִתֵּן	v, G, impf, juss, 3, m, s √נתן "may he give" On the jussive as blessing, see Berg 2 §10h.
יְהוָה	DN "YHWH"
לָכֶם	prep לְ w/ 2, m, pl, gen sx "to you" On masculine suffixes referring to feminine substantives, see GKC §135o, Brock §124b, Joüon §149b, and Wms §234.
וּמְצֶאןָ	v, G, impf, impv, 2, f, pl √מצא w/ וּ conj "that you will find" On the form, see Berg 2 §5a, 2 §29c, and GKC §46f. According to GKC §74h, Qimḥi reads מְצֶ֣אןָ; GKC §110i: "The imperative, when depending (with *wāw* copulative) upon a jussive (cohortative), or an interrogative sentence, frequently expresses also a consequence which is to be expected with certainty, and often a consequence which is intended, or in fact an intention." Joüon §177h: "Somtimes a clause introduced by the *wāw* is equivalent to an object clause [§157b]: ... Ruth 1:9 *That YHWH give you to find.*" The volitive sequences are discussed in Lambdin §107, Seow, p. 244 (who translates this as "May YHWH grant *that you may find* a resting place"), and Vance §16.7. A jussive plus an imperative (with simple *wāw*) often expresses a result or purpose clause (i.e., *that* or *so that*)
מְנוּחָה	n, f, s, abs מְנוּחָה √נוח "resting place, rest"
אִשָּׁה	n, f, s, abs אִשָּׁה √אנש "woman [≈ each]"
בֵּית	n, m, s, cs בַּ֣יִת w/ prep בְּ "in the house of" As here, before the word בַּ֣יִת the preposition בְּ often is *apocopated,* that is, "is dropped off." See Joüon §133c.
אִישָׁהּ	n, m, s, *st. pr.* אִישׁ √אנש w/ 3, f, s, gen sx "her husband"
וַתִּשַּׁק	v, G, impf, indic, 3, f, s √נשק w/ וַ cons "and she kissed"
לָהֶן	prep לְ w/ 3, f, pl, gen sx "[to] them"
וַתִּשֶּׂאנָה	v, G, impf, indic, 3, f, pl √נשא w/ וַ cons "and they lifted up" Compare with the form in 1:14.

קוֹלָן n, m, s, *st. pr.* קוֹל √קול w/ 3, f, pl, gen sx "their voice"
According to Joüon §136l, there is a tendency to use a singular instead of a plural where several individuals have similar things, such as *voice* here.

וַתִּבְכֶּינָה v, G, impf, indic, 3, f, pl √בכה w/ ו cons "and they wept"

1:10 וַתֹּאמַרְנָה־לָּהּ כִּי־אִתָּךְ נָשׁוּב לְעַמֵּךְ׃

1:10　They said to her, "We will return with you to your people!"

וַתֹּאמַרְנָה־ v, G, impf, indic, 3, f, pl √אמר w/ ו cons "and they said"

לָּהּ prep לְ w/ 3, f, s, gen sx "to her"

כִּי־ conj כִּי "that, for, when"
N.B.: כִּי often introduces a direct quote much as לֵאמֹר does.

אִתָּךְ prep אֵת w/ 2, f, s, gen sx "with you"

נָשׁוּב v, G, impf, indic, 1, c, pl √שוב "we will return"

לְעַמֵּךְ n, m, s, *st. pr.* עָם √עמם w/ prep לְ and 2, f, s, gen sx "to your people"

1:11 וַתֹּאמֶר נָעֳמִי שֹׁבְנָה בְנֹתַי לָמָּה תֵלַכְנָה עִמִּי הַעֽוֹד־לִי בָנִים בְּמֵעַי וְהָיוּ לָכֶם לַאֲנָשִׁים׃

1:11　Naomi said, "Return, my daughters! Why would you go with me? Do I still have sons in my womb who could be husbands for you?"

וַתֹּאמֶר v, G, impf, indic, 3, f, s √אמר w/ ו cons "and she said"

נָעֳמִי PN "Naomi"

שֹׁבְנָה v, G, impf, impv, 2, f, pl √שוב "return!"

בְנֹתַי n, f, pl, *st. pr.* בַּת √בנה? w/ 1, c, s, gen sx "my daughters"

לָמָּה interr pron מָה "what?" w/ prep לְ "to" meaning "for what?" = "why?"

תֵלַכְנָה v, G, impf, indic, 2, f, pl √הלך "you will walk"
According to Joüon §113n, the imperfect can have a nuance of "want to," here "Why *would you want to come* with me?" *BHRG* §19.3.5: "The imperfect can be

used to indicate one of the following modalities: … (ii) The *(un)desirability* of events," and they translate our clause: "Why *do* you *want to go* with me?"

עִמִּי — prep עִם √עמם w/ 1, c, s, gen sx "with me"

הַעוֹד־ — temp adv עוֹד w/ interr ה "still?"

לִי — prep לְ w/ 1, c, s, gen sx "to me"

בָנִים — n, m, pl, abs בֵּן √בנה? "sons"

בְּמֵעַי — n, m, *pl. tan., st. pr.* מֵעֶה √מעה w/ prep בְּ and 1, c, s, gen sx "in my internal organs, inward parts (intestines, bowels), belly [≈ womb]"

וְהָיוּ — v, G, pf, 3, c, pl √היה w/ ו cons "that they will be"
GKC §112e: "The perfect consecutive in immediate dependence on the preceding tense, or its equivalent, serves … [§112p] to express *future* actions … as the temporal or logical consequence of tenses, or their equivalents, which announce or require such future actions or events. Thus—(a) After imperfects in the sense of a simple future…; and in interrogative sentences." *IBHS* §32.2.4a says, "The *wəqataltí* form after nominal clauses shows the same range of meanings as after suffix-conjugation forms: … in a consequent situation," and they translate our clause "Do I still have sons in my womb *that* they *may become* husbands for you?" So also Joüon §119i n. 2. Driver, p. 132, equating our clause to an imperfect with interrogative ה (here הַעוֹד־לִי) followed by a perfect with *wāw* consecutive (here וְהָיוּ), translates Ruth 1:11 as a result clause: "*have* I still sons in my womb והיו *and will* they be (= for them to be) to you for husbands?"

לָכֶם — prep לְ w/ 2, m, pl, gen sx "to you"
On masculine suffixes referring to feminine substantives, see GKC §135o, Brock §124b, Joüon §149b, and Wms §234.

לַאֲנָשִׁים — n, m, pl, abs, אִישׁ √אנש w/ prep לְ "for husbands"

1:12 שֹׁבְנָה בְנֹתַי לֵכְןָ כִּי זָקַנְתִּי מִהְיוֹת לְאִישׁ כִּי אָמַרְתִּי יֶשׁ־לִי תִקְוָה גַּם הָיִיתִי הַלַּיְלָה לְאִישׁ וְגַם יָלַדְתִּי בָנִים׃

1:12 "Return, my daughters! Go, since I am too old to belong to a husband! For if I said, 'I have hope of both belonging to a husband tonight and bearing sons,'

שֹׁבְנָה — v, G, impf, impv, 2, f, pl √שוב "return!"

בְּנֹתַי | n, f, pl, *st. pr.* בַּת √בנה? w/ 1, c, s, gen sx "my daughters"

לֵכְןָ | v, G, impf, impv, 2, f, pl √הלך "go!"
On the form, see Berg 2 §5a, 2 §26o, and GKC §46f.

כִּי | conj כִּי "that, for, when"

זָקַנְתִּי | v, G, pf, 1, c, s √זקן "I am old"
On the present significance of the perfect here, see Berg 2 §6g.

מִהְיוֹת | v, G, inf, cs √היה w/ prep מִן "from being"
On מִן after an adjective or stative verb with the sense of quantitative difference, see Brock §111g.

לְאִישׁ | n, m, s, abs אִישׁ √אנש? w/ prep לְ "for a man"

כִּי | conj כִּי "that, for, when"
According to Wms §446 and §517, here כִּי introduces an unreal condition (i.e., a hypothetical situation).

אָמַרְתִּי | v, G, pf, 1, c, s √אמר "I said [≈ if I said]"
GKC §106p states that the perfect may be used "to express actions and facts, whose accomplishment in the past is to be represented, not as actual, but only as possible (generally corresponding to the Latin imperfect or pluperfect subjunctive)," and translates our word "*if I should think*." Driver, p. 45, understands this clause as "that I should have said, I have hope."

יֶשׁ־ | part of existence יֵשׁ "there is"
IBHS §4.5b: "In a *verbal clause* the predicate is a verb," which may be a "*finite verb*," an "*infinitive absolute*," an "*infinitive construct*," or a "*quasi-verbal indicator*, which are particles denoting existence." On יֶשׁ־לְ expressing possession, see Seow, p. 108.

לִי | prep לְ w/ 1, c, s, gen sx "to me"

תִקְוָה | n, f, s, abs תִּקְוָה √קוה "hope"

גַּם | adv גַּם √גמם "also"
The Hebrew וְגַם ... גַּם is an idiom for "both ... and."

הָיִיתִי | v, G, pf, 1, c, s √היה "I was"

הַלַּיְלָה | n, f, s, abs לַיְלָה √ליל w/ def art "tonight"

לְאִישׁ | n, m, s, abs אִישׁ √אנש? w/ prep לְ "to a man"

וְגַם | adv גַּם √גמם w/ ו
The Hebrew וְגַם ... גַּם is an idiom for "both ... and."

יָלַ֫דְתִּי	v, G, pf, 1, c, s √ילד "I bore"
בָנִים	n, m, pl, abs בֵּן √בנה? "sons"

1:13 הֲלָהֵן ׀ תְּשַׂבֵּ֫רְנָה עַד אֲשֶׁר יִגְדָּ֫לוּ הֲלָהֵן֙ תֵּֽעָגֵ֔נָה לְבִלְתִּי הֱי֣וֹת לְאִ֑ישׁ אַל בְּנֹתַ֗י כִּֽי־מַר־לִ֤י מְאֹד֙ מִכֶּ֔ם כִּֽי־יָצְאָ֥ה בִ֖י יַד־יְהוָֽה׃

1:13 would you wait for them until they grew up? Would you, for them, shut yourselves off from belonging to a husband? No, my daughters! For it is far more bitter for me than you since the hand of YHWH is against me!"

Note that 1:13 is a continuation of the sentence in 1:12; so also Joüon §15e.

הֲלָהֵן	conj. לָהֵן w/ interr ה "would [you], therefore?" According to GKC §103f n. 4, לָהֵן here is Aramaic "therefore"; so also BL §81f′.
or	
	prep לְ w/ 3, f, pl, gen sx and interr ה "for them?" According to *HALOT* 2:521 (*s.v.* לָהֵן), read here "both times לָהֶם *to wait for them* (meaning her eventual sons)."
תְּשַׂבֵּ֫רְנָה	v, D, impf, indic, 2, f, pl √שבר "would you wait" According to GKC §107x, the imperfect is used in the apodosis.
עַד	prep עַד √עדה "until"
אֲשֶׁר	rel pron אֲשֶׁר √אשר "that"
יִגְדָּ֫לוּ	v, G, impf, indic, 3, c, pl (pausal form) √גדל "they grew up"
הֲלָהֵן֙	prep לְ w/ 3, f, pl, gen sx and interr ה "for them?" See discussion above under first occurrence of this word in this verse.
תֵּֽעָגֵ֔נָה	v, N, impf, indic, 2, f, pl √עגן "would you shut yourselves in" According to GKC §51m, a *pataḥ* is the usual theme vowel in the N stem second and third feminine plural, and a *ṣērê* is found only in תֵּעָגֵ֫נָה here, "from עגן, and hence, with loss of the doubling, for תֵּעָגֵּ֫נָה." See also Berg 2 §5a, 2 §16g, and BL §49v. According to GKC §107x, the imperfect is used in the apodosis.
לְבִלְתִּי	neg part בִּלְתִּי (from בֵּ֫לֶת [√בלה?]; cf. Ugaritic *blt*) w/ לְ used to negate infinitives "not to…"
הֱי֣וֹת	v, G, inf, cs √היה "be" On the gerundival sense of the infinitive here, see Berg 2 §11p.

לְאִישׁ   n, m, s, abs, אִישׁ √אנשׁ? w/ prep לְ "to a husband"

אַל   neg part אַל "no!"
According to GKC §152g, the use of אַל by itself, as here, in the sense of "no, certainly not (like mhV or mh; gevnhtai)" is the result of shortening a full clause; they translate this occurrence of אַל בְּנֹתַי as *"nay, my daughters."* So also Wms §§403, 595 and Joüon §§160j, 161l.

בְּנֹתַי   n, f, pl, *st. pr.* בַּת √בנה? w/ 1, c, s, gen sx "my daughters"

כִּי־   conj כִּי "that, for, when"

מַר־   adj, m, s, abs מַר √מרר "bitter"

לִי   prep לְ w/ 1, c, s, gen sx "to me"
Joüon §152d understands this clause as a neuter construction: "it is bitter for me." Similarly, Brock §35b understands this as an impersonal construction.

מְאֹד   n, m, s, as adv acc מְאֹד √מאד "very, exceedingly; much"

מִכֶּם   prep מִן w/ 2, m (!), pl, gen sx "than [for] you"
IBHS §14.4f: "It is sometimes difficult to distinguish between a positive comparison and a comparison of capability." They offer these translations: "I am *much too bitter* for you. / I have *more bitterness than* you." Joüon §141i opts for the first understanding.

כִּי־   conj כִּי "that, for, when"

יָצְאָה   v, G, pf, 3, f, s √יצא "she went out"

בִי   prep בְּ w/ 1, c, s, gen sx "against me"

יַד־   n, f, s, cs יָד "the hand of"

יְהוָה   DN "YHWH"

1:14 וַתִּשֶּׂנָה קוֹלָן וַתִּבְכֶּינָה עוֹד וַתִּשַּׁק עָרְפָּה לַחֲמוֹתָהּ וְרוּת דָּבְקָה בָּהּ:

1:14 They lifted up their voice and wept again; Orpah kissed her mother-in-law, but Ruth stuck with her.

וַתִּשֶּׂנָה   v, G, impf, indic, 3, f, pl √נשׂא w/ ו cons "and they lifted up"
According to GKC §74k, a quiescent א is often omitted in writing, such as in the imperfect תִּשֶּׂנָה," listing our verse as an example. So also Berg 2 §29d and Joüon §78c. GKC §76b lists וַתִּשֶּׂנָה as a difficult form (תִּשֶּׂאנָה is the expected

form). BL §59c states that our text is the K of the Western texts ("nach den Okzidentalen") against a Q תִּשֶּׂאנָה, which is also the K in the Eastern texts ("nach den Orientalen auch im Kt.")

קוֹלָן	n, m, s, *st. pr.* קוֹל√ w/ 3, f, pl, gen sx "their voice"
וַתִּבְכֶּינָה	v, G, impf, indic, 3, f, pl בכה√ w/ ו cons "and they wept"
עוֹד	subst as adv acc עוד√ "again"
וַתִּשַּׁק	v, G, impf, indic, 3, f, s נשק√ w/ ו cons "and she kissed"
עָרְפָּה	PN "Orpah"
לַחֲמוֹתָה	n, f, s, *st. pr.* חמות√ חמה w/ 3, f, s, gen sx and prep לְ "her mother-in-law"
וְרוּת	PN w/ ו disj "but Ruth"
דָּבְקָה בָּהּ	v, G, pf, 3, f, s דבק√ w/ prep בְּ and 3, f, s, gen sx "she stuck with her" The root דבק with the preposition בְּ means "to stick to, cling to." On the perfect after the imperfect in a contrastive situation, see Joüon §118f.

1:15 וַתֹּאמֶר הִנֵּה שָׁבָה יְבִמְתֵּךְ אֶל־עַמָּהּ וְאֶל־אֱלֹהֶיהָ שׁוּבִי אַחֲרֵי יְבִמְתֵּךְ:

1:15 She said, "Look, your sister-in-law has turned back to her people and to her gods. Turn back after your sister-in-law!"

וַתֹּאמֶר	v, G, impf, indic, 3, f, s אמר√ w/ ו cons "and she said"
הִנֵּה	dem part הִנֵּה "behold"
שָׁבָה	v, G, pf, 3, f, s שוב√ "she has returned"
יְבִמְתֵּךְ	n, f, s, *st. pr.* יְבֶמֶת יבם√ w/ 2, f, s, gen sx "your sister-in-law"
אֶל־	prep אֶל "to"
עַמָּהּ	n, m, s, *st. pr.* עַם עממ√ w/ 3, f, s, gen sx "her people"
וְאֶל־	prep אֶל "to" w/ ו conj "and to"
אֱלֹהֶיהָ	n, m, pl, *st. pr.* אֱלֹהִים אלה√ w/ 3, f, s, gen sx "her gods"
שׁוּבִי	v, G, impf, impv, 2, f, s שוב√ "Return!"
אַחֲרֵי	prep "behind, after" (properly n, m, pl, cs אַחַר אחר√ "hinder parts of")
יְבִמְתֵּךְ	n, f, s, *st. pr.* יְבֶמֶת יבם√ w/ 2, f, s, gen sx "your sister-in-law"

1:16 וַתֹּאמֶר רוּת אַל־תִּפְגְּעִי־בִי לְעָזְבֵךְ לָשׁוּב מֵאַחֲרָיִךְ כִּי אֶל־אֲשֶׁר תֵּלְכִי אֵלֵךְ וּבַאֲשֶׁר תָּלִינִי אָלִין עַמֵּךְ עַמִּי וֵאלֹהַיִךְ אֱלֹהָי:

1:16   Ruth said, "Stop urging me to abandon you, to turn back from you! For wherever you go, I will go, and wherever you lodge, I will lodge. Your people will be my people, and your God will be my God."

וַתֹּאמֶר	v, G, impf, indic, 3, f, s √אמר w/ ו cons "and she said"
רוּת	PN "Ruth"
אַל־תִּפְגְּעִי־	v, G, impf, juss, 2, f, s √פגע w/ neg part אַל "stop urging"
בִי	prep בְּ w/ 1, c, s, gen sx "me"
לְעָזְבֵךְ	v, G, inf, cs √עזב w/ prep לְ and 2, f, s, acc sx "to leave you" Since a pronominal suffix attached to an infinitive construct may be subjective or objective, only the context can determine which it is; see Seow, pp. 255–56.
לָשׁוּב	v, G, inf, cs √שוב w/ prep לְ "to return"
מֵאַחֲרָיִךְ	prep "behind, after" (properly n, m, pl, cs אַחַר √אחר "hinder parts of") w/ prep מִן "from" w/ 2, f, s, gen sx "from after you"
כִּי	conj כִּי "that, for, when"
אֶל־	prep אֶל "to"
אֲשֶׁר	rel pron אֲשֶׁר √אשר "that" = "wherever" See GKC §138e on this use of אֲשֶׁר.
תֵּלְכִי	v, G, impf, indic, 2, f, s √הלך "you go"
אֵלֵךְ	v, G, impf, indic, 1, c, s √הלך "I will go"
וּבַאֲשֶׁר	rel pron אֲשֶׁר √אשר "that" w/ prep בְּ and ו conj "and in that" = "wherever" On אֲשֶׁר with בְּ in this sense, see Joüon §158m.
תָּלִינִי	v, G, impf, indic, 2, f, s √לין "you lodge"
אָלִין	v, G, impf, indic, 1, c, s √לין "I will lodge"
עַמֵּךְ	n, m, s, *st. pr.* עַם √עמם w/ 2, f, s, gen sx "your people"
עַמִּי	n, m, s, *st. pr.* עַם √עמם w/ 1, c, s, gen sx "my people"
וֵאלֹהַיִךְ	n, m, s, *st. pr.* אֱלֹהִים √אלה w/ 2, f, s, gen sx and ו conj "and your God"
אֱלֹהָי	n, m, s, *st. pr.* אֱלֹהִים √אלה w/ 1, c, s, gen sx "my God"

1:17 בַּאֲשֶׁר תָּמוּתִי אָמוּת וְשָׁם אֶקָּבֵר כֹּה יַעֲשֶׂה יְהוָה לִי וְכֹה יֹסִיף כִּי הַמָּוֶת יַפְרִיד בֵּינִי וּבֵינֵךְ׃

1:17 "Wherever you die, I will die, and there I will be buried. Thus will YHWH do to me and thus will he add, when death separates you from me!"

בַּאֲשֶׁר	rel pron אֲשֶׁר √אשר "that" w/ prep בְּ "in that" = "wherever" *IBHS* §19.2b: "The most common relative pronoun, אשר, is etymologically a locative noun, 'a step, place,' and may be considered a noun always used in the construct. There is no trace of the etymological sense." But in n. 4 they add, "Save *perhaps* in Judg 5:27; Ruth 1:17 is dubious."
תָּמוּתִי	v, G, impf, indic, 2, f, s √מות "you die"
אָמוּת	v, G, impf, indic, 1, c, s √מות "I will die"
וְשָׁם	loc adv שָׁם w/ ו conj "and there"
אֶקָּבֵר	v, N, impf, indic, 1, c, s √קבר "I will be buried"
כֹּה	dem adv כֹּה "thus"
יַעֲשֶׂה	v, G, impf, indic, 3, m, s √עשה "he will do" Morphologically, this form cannot be a jussive (which would be יַעַשׂ), nor is it required by the context. Berg 2 §101m: "Along with the imperative and the jussive, the simple imperfect, in both the second and third persons, can also be used for the expression of requests." *IBHS* 31.5b adds that the volitional forms (e.g., a jussive) "emphasize the will of the speaker, whereas the non-perfectives [as here] … emphasize the action enjoined or forbidden."
יְהוָה	DN "YHWH"
לִי	prep לְ w/ 1, c, s, gen sx "to me"
וְכֹה	dem adv כֹּה w/ ו conj "and thus"
יֹסִיף	v, H, impf, indic, 3, m, s √יסף "he will add"
כִּי	conj כִּי "that, for, when" Every major English translation understands כִּי here as the *if* of a protasis (the *if* part of an if-then clause), translating the clause, "if death separates me from you." Alternatively, one may see כִּי as introducing a temporal clause modifying the apodosis (the *then* part of a conditional clause) and the protasis is left unexpressed (an ellipsis, hence the punctuation in the translation). It is not uncommon in the Bible for an oath to omit either the protasis or the apodosis,

either of which can usually be deduced from the context (see further Wms §§596–97 and *IBHS* §40.2.2). In this case, the protasis would be something like "if I do not do what I just said." On imprecation and swearing clauses, see Joüon §165.

הַמָּ֫וֶת	n, m, s, abs מָ֫וֶת √מות w/ def art "the death"
יַפְרִיד	v, H, impf, indic, 3, m, s √פרד "he will separate"
בֵּינִי	subs cs בֵּין "interval, space between," always as prep בֵּין √בין w/ 1, c, s, gen sx "between me"
וּבֵינֵךְ	subs cs בֵּין "interval, space between," always as prep בֵּין √בין w/ 2, f, s, gen sx and ו conj "and between you"

1:18 וַתֵּ֫רֶא כִּי־מִתְאַמֶּ֫צֶת הִיא לָלֶ֫כֶת אִתָּהּ וַתֶּחְדַּל לְדַבֵּר אֵלֶ֫יהָ:

1:18 She saw that she was determined to go with her, so she ceased speaking to her.

וַתֵּ֫רֶא	v, G, impf, indic, 3, f, s √ראה w/ ו cons "and she saw"
כִּי־	conj כִּי "that, for, when"
מִתְאַמֶּ֫צֶת	v, tD, ptc, f, s, abs √אמץ "determined"
הִיא	indep pers pron, 3, f, s הִיא "she"
לָלֶ֫כֶת	v, G, inf, cs √הלך w/ prep לְ "to go"
אִתָּהּ	prep אֵת w/ 3, f, s, gen sx "with her"
וַתֶּחְדַּל	v, G, impf, indic, 3, f, s √חדל w/ ו cons "so she ceased"
לְדַבֵּר	v, D, inf, cs √דבר w/ prep לְ "to speak" *IBHS* 36.2.3b explains, "Infinitives with *l* can … serve as *verbal complements*, supplying a verb to 'complete' the main finite verb…. Some finite verbs generally govern complements in לְ…, while others can govern infinitives with or without לְ."
אֵלֶ֫יהָ	prep אֶל w/ 3, f, gen sx "to her"

1:19 וַתֵּלַכְנָה שְׁתֵּיהֶם עַד־בֹּאָנָה בֵּית לָחֶם וַיְהִי כְּבֹאָנָה בֵּית לֶחֶם וַתֵּהֹם כָּל־הָעִיר עֲלֵיהֶן וַתֹּאמַרְנָה הֲזֹאת נָעֳמִי:

1:19 The two of them kept going until they came to Bethlehem. When they came to Bethlehem, the whole city was in an uproar over them, and the women said, "Is this Naomi?"

וַתֵּלַכְנָה	v, G, impf, indic, 3, f, pl √הלך w/ ו cons "and they went"
שְׁתֵּיהֶם	n, f, du, *st. pr.* שְׁתַּיִם (m, שְׁנַיִם) √שנה w/ 3, m, pl, gen sx "the two of them" Read הֶן (third feminine plural genitive suffix) with many MSS; cf. BL §79c.
עַד־	prep עַד √עדה "until"
בֹּאָנָה	v, G, inf, cs √בוא w/ 3, f, pl, gen sx "their coming" The form of the genitive suffix נָה ֶ is a variant of the standard ן ָ (see BL §29p and GKC §91f). Joüon §94h suggests that the variant is for assonance.
בֵּית לָחֶם	GN "Bethlehem"
וַיְהִי	v, G, impf, indic, 3, m, s √היה w/ ו cons "and it was"
כְּבֹאָנָה	v, G, inf, cs √בוא w/ 3, f, pl, gen sx and w/ prep כְּ "when they came" On this form of the genitive suffix, see above in this verse under בֹּאָנָה.
בֵּית לֶחֶם	GN "Bethlehem"
וַתֵּהֹם	v, N, impf, indic, 3, f, s √הום w/ ו cons "and she [the city] was in an uproar" So BDB *s.v.* √הום, who reference GKC §72v; HALOT *s.v.* √הום agrees (and translates the form as "go wild"). But, some understand the form as: v, G, impf, indic, 3, f, s √המה w/ ו cons "and she [the city] was abuzz" So Berg 2 §31f, who says that this form, "though meant as N stem of a II-*w* or a geminate root, is to be read as a form from √המה."
כָּל־	n, m, s, cs כֹּל √כלל "all of"
הָעִיר	n, f, s, abs עִיר w/ def art "the city"
עֲלֵיהֶן	prep עַל √עלה "over" w/ 3, f, pl, gen sx "over them"
וַתֹּאמַרְנָה	v, G, impf, indic, 3, f, pl √אמר w/ ו cons "and they said" According to Joüon §155b n. 3 (see also §155e n. 1), the indefinite personal subject is usually expressed by the third masculine plural form of the verb. The feminine gender here indicates that only the women of the city are meant in this verse.

הֲזֹאת	dem pron, prox, f, s זֹאת (m זֶה) w/ interr ה "is this?" Joüon §161b understands the ה as emphatic here rather than as an interrogative: "This is Naomi!"
נָעֳמִי	PN "Naomi"

1:20 וַתֹּאמֶר אֲלֵיהֶן אַל־תִּקְרֶאנָה לִי נָעֳמִי קְרֶאןָ לִי מָרָא כִּי־הֵמַר שַׁדַּי לִי מְאֹד:

1:20 She said to them, "Do not call me 'Naomi,' call me 'Mara' for the Almighty has greatly embittered me!"

וַתֹּאמֶר	v, G, impf, indic, 3, f, s √אמר w/ ו cons "and she said"
אֲלֵיהֶן	prep אֶל w/ 3, f, pl, gen sx "to them"
אַל־	neg part אַל "not"
תִּקְרֶאנָה	v, G, impf, juss, 2, f, pl √קרא (w/ neg part) "don't call" *or* "stop calling"
לִי	prep לְ w/ 1, c, s, gen sx "to me"
נָעֳמִי	PN "Naomi"
קְרֶאןָ	v, G, impf, impv, 2, f, pl √קרא "call" On the form, see Berg 2 §5a, 2 §29c, and GKC §46f. According to GKC §74h, Qimḥi reads קְרֶאןָ.
לִי	prep לְ w/ 1, c, s, gen sx "to me"
מָרָא	PN "Mara" This is a variant of the feminine singular absolute adjective מָרָה from מַר √מרר "bitter." GKC §80h explain, "אָ, the Aramaic orthography for הָ, [is a rare feminine ending occurring] chiefly in the later writers." So also BL §62x (see also §74h′). Joüon §89k simply lists this as a rare feminine form.
כִּי־	conj כִּי "that, for, when"
הֵמַר	v, H, pf, 3, m, s √מרר "he embittered"
שַׁדַּי	DN "Almighty" The etymology is unknown, perhaps related to Akkadian *šadū,* "mountain."
לִי	prep לְ w/ 1, c, s, gen sx "to me"
מְאֹד	n, m, s, as adv acc מְאֹד √מאד "very, exceedingly; much"

1:21 אֲנִי מְלֵאָה הָלַכְתִּי וְרֵיקָם הֱשִׁיבַנִי יְהוָה לָמָּה תִקְרֶאנָה לִי נָעֳמִי וַיהוָה עָנָה בִי וְשַׁדַּי הֵרַע לִי:

1:21 "As for me, I left full, but YHWH has made me return empty. Why should you call me Naomi, when YHWH has oppressed me and the Almighty has done evil to me?"

אֲנִי	indep pers pron, 1, c, s אֲנִי "as for me"
מְלֵאָה	adj, f, s, abs מָלֵא √מלא "full" GKC §118m–n (and §100g) identifies this as an adverbial accusative of the adjective parallel with the adverb רֵיקָם. So similarly, Joüon §126a. See also *GAHG* 3:146 n. 382.
הָלַכְתִּי	v, G, pf, 1, c, s √הלך "I walked"
וְרֵיקָם	adv רֵיקָם √ריק w/ ו disj "but emptily, vainly" GKC §100g: "Some adverbs are formed by the addition of formative syllables (most frequently ־ָם) to substantives or adjectives, e.g. … רֵיקָם *in vain, frustra*, but also *empty* (from רֵיק *empty, emptiness, vanum*)," noting that here it is "parallel with the *fem* מְלֵאָה *full*."
הֱשִׁיבַנִי	v, H, pf, 3, m, s √שוב w/ 1, c, s, acc sx "he made me return"
יְהוָה	DN "YHWH"
לָמָּה	interr מָה "what?" w/ prep לְ "to" = "why"
תִקְרֶאנָה	v, G, impf, indic, 2, f, pl √קרא "should you call" or "do you call"
לִי	prep לְ w/ 1, c, s, gen sx "to me"
נָעֳמִי	PN "Naomi"
וַיהוָה	DN w/ ו conj "and YHWH" Driver, p. 197: "In the translation of circumstantial clauses there is considerable scope for variety. Sometimes the ו may be rendered most simply and naturally *and*—the subordinate position of the fact thus introduced being manifest from the sense of the passage; but at other times it will be better, precisely as in the case of the participle in Greek or Latin, to make the meaning more evident by the adoption of some circumlocution such as *if, when, although, as, since*, etc., as the context requires." As an example, on p. 198 he translates our clause: "Why call ye me Naomi וַיהוָה עָנָה בִי *when* or *seeing* Yahweh hath testified against me?"

עָנָה — v, G, pf, 3, m, s √ענה "he answered; he testified"
I suggest reading עִנָּה, the D perfect third masculine singular of ענהIII ("he oppressed"), but Driver, p. 198, translates it "testified."

בִּי — prep בְּ w/ 1, c, s, gen sx "in me; against me"

וְשַׁדַּי — DN w/ ו conj "and the Almighty"
Etymology is unknown, perhaps related to Akkadian *šadū*, "mountain."

הֵרַע — v, H, pf, 3, m, s √רעע "he did evil"

לִי — prep לְ w/ 1, c, s, gen sx "to me"

1:22 וַתָּשָׁב נָעֳמִי וְרוּת הַמּוֹאֲבִיָּה כַלָּתָהּ עִמָּהּ הַשָּׁבָה מִשְּׂדֵי מוֹאָב וְהֵמָּה בָּאוּ בֵּית לֶחֶם בִּתְחִלַּת קְצִיר שְׂעֹרִים:

1:22 Naomi returned and Ruth, the Moabitess, her daughter-in-law who returned with her from the region of Moab; but they came to Bethlehem at the beginning of the barley harvest.

וַתָּשָׁב — v, G, impf, indic, 3, f, s, √שוב w/ ו cons "and she returned"
Joüon §118i: "The *wayyiqtol* is used also for a conclusion or a recapitulation: ... Ruth 1:22."

נָעֳמִי — PN "Naomi"

וְרוּת — PN w/ ו conj "and Ruth"

הַמּוֹאֲבִיָּה — gent adj, f, s, abs מוֹאֲבִיָּה (m, s מוֹאָבִי) w/ def art "the Moabitess"

כַלָּתָהּ — n, f, s, *st. pr.* כַּלָּה √כלל w/ 3, f, s, gen sx "her daughter-in-law"

עִמָּהּ — prep עִם √עמם w/ 3, f, s, gen sx "with her"

הַשָּׁבָה — v, G, pf, 3, f, s √שוב w/ def art, "who returned," but read הַשָּׁבָה (i.e., accent on last syllable), v, G, ptc, act, f, sg, abs √שוב w/ def art, "who returned"
According to GKC §138k, even though the Masorah requires הַשָּׁבָה be parsed as a perfect (because of the tone on the first syllable; see also Vance §11.2.5) and in spite of the fact that the definite article (functioning as a relative pronoun; see GKC §138g) with a perfect is not unheard of, the author probably intended a participle, which requires only shifting the accent to the end of the word (so also Joüon §145e). *IBHS* §19.7d: "However the

pointing or accentuation in the Masorah is to be explained, such forms should probably be read as participles…; the article with the perfective is unlikely in early texts."

מִשְּׂדֵי   n, m, pl, cs שָׂדֶה √שדה w/ prep מִן "from [the] fields of = from the region of"

מוֹאָב   GN "Moab"

וְהֵמָּה   indep pers pron, 3, m, pl הֵמָּה w/ ו disj "but they"
Read הֵנָּה, a third feminine plural independent personal pronoun, "they." In contrast, GKC §32n: "In some passages הֵמָּה stands for the feminine," listing our verse as an example. See also §BL 28j. Joüon §149c simply says that the supplanting of the feminine by the masculine in independent personal pronouns is very rare and occurs only in the third plural.

בָּאוּ   v, G, pf, 3, c, pl √בוא "they came"

בֵּית לֶחֶם   GN "Bethlehem"
IBHS §10.2.2b n. 15: "the *b* is omitted before *byt lḥm* in Ruth 1:22"; see also §10.2.2b n. 14: "It is frequently suggested that the preposition *b* is omitted before the words *ptḥ* 'entrance' and *byt* 'house' by haplology, i.e., the tendency to avoid two similar sounds (here, bilabial stops) or syllables next to one another; see, e.g., Joüon §126h / p. 380. (Haplology, a phonological process, should not be confused with haplography, a scribal process, though they may have the same effect in a written text. Haplology is best exemplified in English by the avoidance of '-lily' words, e.g., there is no adverb from 'friendly' of the form 'friendlily.') S. R. Driver explains the phenomenon syntactically: 'by custom the use of the accus[ative] to express rest in a place is restricted to cases in which *a noun in the genitive follows*'; see *Notes on the Hebrew Text and the Topography of the Books of Samuel* (Oxford: Clarendon, 1913) 37 n. 2; cf., however, [*IBHS* §10.2.2b] ## 2–3."

בִּתְחִלַּת   n, f, s, cs תְּחִלָּה √חלל w/ prep בְּ "at [the] beginning of"

קְצִיר   n, m, s, cs קָצִיר √קצר "[the] harvesting, harvest of"

שְׂעֹרִים   n, f, pl, abs שְׂעֹרָה √שער "barley"

RUTH 2:1–23

2:1 וּלְנָעֳמִ֞י מְיֻדָּ֣ע [מוֹדַ֣ע] לְאִישָׁ֗הּ אִ֚ישׁ גִּבּ֣וֹר חַ֔יִל מִמִּשְׁפַּ֖חַת אֱלִימֶ֑לֶךְ וּשְׁמ֖וֹ בֹּֽעַז׃

2:1   Now Naomi had a kinsman on her husband's side, a powerful man of wealth from the family of Elimelech, whose name was Boaz.

וּלְנָעֳמִ֞י	PN w/ prep לְ and ו disj "now there was to Naomi"

According to *IBHS* §39.2.3c, a disjunctive *wāw* "at the beginning of a story episode," may be used when new characters are first mentioned. They thus translate our passage: "*Now*, Naomi had a relative on her husband's side … named Boaz" (see also Vance §11.3).

מְיֻדָּע	K, v, Dp, ptc, m, s, abs √ידע "one known [≈ relative]"
מוֹדַע	Q, n, m, s, cs מֹדַע √ידע "kinsman, relative"

It is tempting to treat this as a masculine singular construct Hp participle of ידע, but Hp participles of I-ו roots have a וּ, not a וֹ (i.e., מוּדָע). So it is better treated as a noun (so also Berg 2 §26*i*). Contrast this form מוֹדַע with that of Ruth 3:2, מֹדַעַת (Joüon §89b). The construct state here is impossible, since it is followed by the preposition לְ, so BDB lists an alternate absolute form מוֹדַע, but this seems improbable for two reasons. First, the morphology of Classical Hebrew calls for a long vowel in the accented syllable of a noun in the absolute state (see Vance §4.6.1); second, this is precisely what we find in Prov 7:4b (וּמֹדָע לַבִּינָה תִקְרָא: ["and call understanding 'kinsman!'"]), where מֹדָע is also followed by the preposition לְ. *HALOT* lists מֹדָע as a noun meaning "(distant) relative," citing Ugaritic *mūdū* and Akkadian *mūdū*, both meaning "companion." We should probably simply read מוֹדַע, a form that is to be preferred over מֹדַע, since this is most likely a *mēm*-preformative noun from *√wdᶜ (see BL §61dz): *mawdaᶜ → môdaᶜ* (monopthongization of the *aw* diphthong) → *môdā̆ᶜ* (lengthening of the tonic vowel). See also BL §69b.

לְאִישָׁהּ	n, m, s, *st. pr.* אִישׁ √אנשׁ? w/ 3, f, s, gen sx and w/ prep לְ "belonging to her husband" *IBHS* §11.2.10f: "An *l* phrase must be used if the phrase must unambiguously refer to an indefinite"; they translate our clause: "Naomi had a relative *of* her husband's."
אִישׁ	n, m, s, abs אִישׁ √אנשׁ? "a man"
גִּבּוֹר	n, m, s, cs גִּבּוֹר √גבר "a mighty man of"
חַיִל	n, m, s, abs חַיִל √חול "strength, efficiency, wealth, army"
מִמִּשְׁפַּחַת	n, f, s, cs מִשְׁפָּחָה √שׁפח w/ prep מִן "from [the] family of"
אֱלִימֶלֶךְ	PN "Elimelech"
וּשְׁמוֹ	n, m, s, *st. pr.* שֵׁם w/ 3, m, s, gen sx and וּ conj "and his name"
בֹּעַז	PN "Boaz"

2:2 וַתֹּאמֶר רוּת הַמּוֹאֲבִיָּה אֶל־נָעֳמִי אֵלְכָה־נָּא הַשָּׂדֶה וַאֲלַקֳטָה בַשִּׁבֳּלִים אַחַר אֲשֶׁר אֶמְצָא־חֵן בְּעֵינָיו וַתֹּאמֶר לָהּ לְכִי בִתִּי:

2:2 Ruth, the Moabitess, said to Naomi, "I am going to go to the field so that I may glean among the grain behind him in whose eyes I should find favor." She said to her, "Go, my daughter."

וַתֹּאמֶר	v, G, impf, indic, 3, f, s √אמר w/ וַ cons "and she said"
רוּת	PN "Ruth"
הַמּוֹאֲבִיָּה	gent adj, f, s, abs מוֹאֲבִיָּה (m, s מוֹאָבִי) w/ def art "the Moabitess"
אֶל־	prep אֶל "to"
נָעֳמִי	PN "Naomi"
אֵלְכָה־נָּא	v, G, impf, coh, 1, c, s √הלך w/ part of entreaty "I am going to go" The sense of the particle of entreaty with the cohortative here could be simply asking for permission; so Joüon §114d, who suggests "let me go"; so also *BHRG* §19.4.3 (i) b. On the other hand, instead of asking permission, the sense could be that of suggesting an idea for discussion, which, in addition to the

way I have translated it above, could also be rendered in English as a question: "Why don't I go…?" *BHS* and the printed editions have a simple *shewa* under the לֹ (אֵלְכָה) instead of the *ḥāṭēp pataḥ* of *BHL*. L is very difficult to make out, but it is clear that it is not a simple *shewa*. On L's use of *ḥāṭēp pataḥ,* see *BHL,* xiii–xiv.

הַשָּׂדֶ֖ה   n, m, s, abs שָׂדֶה √שׂדה w/ def art "[to] the field"

וַאֲלַקֳטָה   v, D, impf, coh, 1, c, s √לקט w/ ו conj "that I might glean"
On this sense of the cohortative after an earlier one, see Joüon §114n (cf. §119j). Of course, one could simply continue the nuance of the first cohortative: "and I am going to glean." On the contrast between this verse and the similar expression in Ruth 2:7, see Joüon §122c. The *ḥāṭēp qāmeṣ* may be found under a consonant that should have a *dagesh forte* but does not, especially if the consonant is an emphatic (such as the ק here); so GKC §10h (see also §64i) and Berg 1 §21aa. *BHL* indicates in appendix A that L has an inexplicable *dagesh forte* in the ט (וַאֲלַקֳטָה). Since Classical Hebrew morphology does not permit a vocal *shewa* in a closed syllable (see Vance §2.4.4.4 and §2.13), one must conclude that L's reading is a scribal error.

בַּשִּׁבֳּלִים   n, f, pl, abs שִׁבֹּלֶת √שׁבל w/ prep בְּ "among the ears of grain"
L has בַּשְׁבֳּלִים (that is, a *dagesh* in the preposition ב, but not in the שׁ, noted in appendix A of *BHL*), which *BHL* has corrected to the form used here (as does *BHS* and the printed editions). There should be no *dagesh lene* in the ב (since it is preceded by the vowel at the end of the preceding word, וַאֲלַקֳטָה), but there should be a *dagesh forte* in the שׁ because of the presence of the definite article (the intervocalic ה—between the vocal *shewa* of the preposition בְּ and the *pataḥ* of the definite artice—has elided; see further Vance §7.2).

אַחַ֫ר   loc adv אַחַר √אחר *or* prep "behind, after"

אֲשֶׁר   rel pron אֲשֶׁר √אשר "who"

אֶמְצָא־   v, G, impf, indic, 1, c, s √מצא "I should find favor"

חֵן   n, m, s, abs חֵן √חנן "favor, grace"

בְּעֵינָיו   n, f, du, cs עַיִן √עין w/ 3, m, s, gen sx and prep בְּ "in his eyes"

וַתֹּאמֶר   v, G, impf, indic, 3, f, s √אמר w/ ו cons "and she said"

לָהּ   prep לְ w/ 3, f, s, gen sx "to her"

לְכִי   v, G, impf, impv, 2, f, s √הלך "go!"

בִתִּי   n, f, s, *st. pr.* בַּת √בנה? w/ 1, c, s, gen sx "my daughter"

2:3 וַתֵּלֶךְ וַתָּבוֹא וַתְּלַקֵּט בַּשָּׂדֶה אַחֲרֵי הַקֹּצְרִים וַיִּקֶר מִקְרֶהָ חֶלְקַת הַשָּׂדֶה לְבֹעַז אֲשֶׁר מִמִּשְׁפַּחַת אֱלִימֶלֶךְ:

2:3 She left, and she came and gleaned in the field behind the harvesters—it just so happened to be in the portion of the field that belonged to Boaz, who was of Elimelech's family.

וַתֵּלֶךְ	v, G, impf, indic, 3, f, s √הלך w/ ו cons "and she went"
וַתָּבוֹא	v, G, impf, indic, 3, f, s √בוא w/ ו cons "and she arrived"
וַתְּלַקֵּט	v, D, impf, indic, 3, f, s √לקט w/ ו cons "and she gleaned"
בַּשָּׂדֶה	n, m, s, abs שָׂדֶה√שדה w/ def art and w/ בְּ "in the field"
אַחֲרֵי	prep "behind, after" (properly n, m, pl, cs אַחַר√אחר "hinder parts of")
הַקֹּצְרִים	v, G, act, ptc, m, pl, abs √קצר w/ def art "the harvesters"
וַיִּקֶר	v, G, impf, indic, 3, m, s √קרה w/ ו cons "and it happened" On the form, see Berg 2 §30f. According to *IBHS* §33.2.2a (see also b), this is an example of an "*epexegetical* use of *wayyqtl*," in which "the major fact or situation is stated first, and then the particulars or details, component or concomitant situations are filled in." For Joüon §118k, this is not an idea of succession but of a concomitant circumstance.
מִקְרֶה	n, m, s, abs מִקְרֶה√קרה "accident, chance, fortune" The Hebrew construction וַיִּקֶר מִקְרֶהָ means "it just so happened."
חֶלְקַת	n, f, s, cs חֶלְקָה√חלק "a portion of"
הַשָּׂדֶה	n, m, s, abs, שָׂדֶה√שדה w/ def art "the field"
לְבֹעַז	PN w/ prep לְ "belonging to Boaz" *IBHS* §9.7b: "Periphrastic לְ is also used in cases in which a construct chain [חֶלְקַת הַשָּׂדֶה here] needs to be qualified." GKC §129b: "The introduction of a genitive by לְ sometimes occurs … [§129d] when a genitive is to be made dependent on a nomen regens, which is itself composed of a nomen regens and rectum, and represents, as a compound, one united idea, e.g. [Ruth 2:3] חֶלְקַת הַשָּׂדֶה לְבֹעַז *the portion of field belonging to Boaz* (חֶלְקַת שָׂדֶה בֹעַז would be *the portion of the field of Boaz*)." See also *GAHG* 2:50 n. 233. The point is that Boaz owns the portion of the field, not the whole field.
אֲשֶׁר	rel pron אֲשֶׁר√אשר "who"
מִמִּשְׁפַּחַת	n, f, s, cs מִשְׁפָּחָה√שפח w/ prep מִן "from [the] family of"

אֱלִימֶלֶךְ   PN "Elimelech"

2:4 וְהִנֵּה־בֹעַז בָּא מִבֵּית לֶחֶם וַיֹּאמֶר לַקּוֹצְרִים יְהוָה עִמָּכֶם וַיֹּאמְרוּ לוֹ יְבָרֶכְךָ יְהוָה:

2:4   Now behold, Boaz, coming from Bethlehem, said to the harvesters, "May YHWH be with you!" And they said to him, "May YHWH bless you!"

וְהִנֵּה־	dem part הִנֵּה w/ וֹ disj "now behold"
בֹעַז	PN "Boaz"
בָּא	v, G, act, ptc, m, s, abs √בוא "coming"
or	v, G, pf, 3, m, s √בוא "he came"
מִבֵּית לֶחֶם	GN w/ prep מִן "from Bethlehem"
וַיֹּאמֶר	v, G, impf, indic, 3, m, s √אמר w/ וֹ cons "and he said"
לַקּוֹצְרִים	v, G, act, ptc, m, pl, abs √קצר w/ def art and w/ prep לְ "to the harvesters"
יְהוָה	DN "YHWH"
עִמָּכֶם	prep עִם √עמם w/ 2, m, pl, gen sx "be with you" According to Joüon §163b, a nominal proposition may have an optative sense.
וַיֹּאמְרוּ	v, G, impf, indic, 3, m, pl √אמר w/ וֹ cons "and they said"
לוֹ	prep לְ w/ 3, m, s, gen sx "to him"
יְבָרֶכְךָ	v, D, impf, juss, 3, m, s √ברך w/ 2, m, s, acc sx "may he bless you"
יְהוָה	DN "YHWH"

2:5 וַיֹּאמֶר בֹּעַז לְנַעֲרוֹ הַנִּצָּב עַל־הַקּוֹצְרִים לְמִי הַנַּעֲרָה הַזֹּאת:

2:5   Boaz said to his young man who was stationed over the harvesters, "To whom does this young woman belong?"

וַיֹּאמֶר	v, G, impf, indic, 3, m, s √אמר w/ וֹ cons "and he said"
בֹּעַז	PN "Boaz"

לְנַעֲרוֹ	n, m, s, *st. pr.* נַעַר√נער w/ 3, m, s, gen sx and prep לְ "to his young man"
הַנִּצָּב	v, N, ptc, m, s, abs נצב√ w/ def art "the one stationed"
עַל־	prep עַל√עלה "over"
הַקּוֹצְרִים	v, G, act, ptc, m, pl, abs קצר√ w/ def art "the harvesters"
לְמִי	interr pron מִי w/ prep לְ "to whom?"
הַנַּעֲרָה	n, f, s, abs נַעֲרָה√נער w/ def art "the young woman"
הַזֹּאת	dem adj, prox, f, s זֹאת (m, s, זֶה) w/ def art "this"

2:6 וַיַּעַן הַנַּעַר הַנִּצָּב עַל־הַקּוֹצְרִים וַיֹּאמַר נַעֲרָה מוֹאֲבִיָּה הִיא הַשָּׁבָה עִם־נָעֳמִי מִשְּׂדֵה מוֹאָב:

2:6 The young man stationed over the harvesters answered, "She is a Moabite young woman who returned with Naomi from the region of Moab."

וַיַּעַן	v, G, impf, indic, 3, m, s ענה√ w/ ו cons "and he answered"
הַנַּעַר	n, m, s, abs נַעַר√נער w/ def art "the young man"
הַנִּצָּב	v, N, ptc, m, s, abs נצב√ w/ def art "who was stationed"
עַל־	prep עַל√עלה "over"
הַקּוֹצְרִים	v, G, act, ptc, m, pl, abs קצר√ w/ def art "the harvesters"
וַיֹּאמַר	v, G, impf, indic, 3, m, s אמר√ w/ ו cons "and he said"
נַעֲרָה	n, f, s, abs נַעֲרָה√נער "a young woman"
מוֹאֲבִיָּה	gent adj, f, s, abs מוֹאֲבִיָּה (m, s מוֹאָבִי) "Moabitess"
הִיא	indep pers pron, 3, f, s הִיא "she"
הַשָּׁבָה	v, G, pf, 3, f, s שׁוּב√שׁוב w/ def art "who returned"
	According to GKC §138k, although the Masorah requires that הַשָּׁבָה be parsed as a perfect (because of the tone on the first syllable) and in spite of the fact that the definite article (functioning as a relative pronoun; see GKC §138g) with a perfect is not unheard of, the author probably intended a participle here, which requires only the shifting of the accent to the end of the word; so also Joüon §145e. *IBHS* §19.7d explains, "However the pointing or accentuation in the Masorah is to be explained, such forms

should probably be read as participles; the article with the perfective is unlikely in early texts."

עִם־	prep עִם √עמם "with"
נׇעֳמִי	PN "Naomi"
מִשְּׂדֵה	n, m, s, cs שָׂדֶה √שדה w/ prep מִן "from [the] field of"
מוֹאָב	GN "Moab"

2:7 וַתֹּאמֶר אֲלַקֳטָה־נָּא֙ וְאָסַפְתִּי בָעֳמָרִ֔ים אַחֲרֵי הַקּוֹצְרִ֑ים וַתָּב֣וֹא וַתַּעֲמ֗וֹד מֵאָ֤ז הַבֹּ֙קֶר֙ וְעַד־עַ֔תָּה זֶ֛ה שִׁבְתָּ֥הּ הַבַּ֖יִת מְעָֽט׃

2:7 "She said, 'Please, let me glean and gather among the sheaves behind the harvesters.' She came and stood from then (it was morning) until now. This break of hers inside has been a little one."

וַתֹּאמֶר	v, G, impf, indic, 3, f, s √אמר w/ ו cons "and she said"
אֲלַקֳטָה־נָּא	v, D, impf, coh, 1, c, s √לקט w/ part of entreaty "Please let me glean" The *ḥāṭēp qāmeṣ* may be found under a consonant that should have a *dagesh forte* but does not, especially if the consonant is an emphatic (such as the ק here); so GKC §10h (see also §64i) and Berg 1 §21aa.
וְאָסַפְתִּי	v, G, pf, 1, c, s √אסף w/ ו cons "and gather" IBHS §32.2.2a: "*Wəqataltí* [note the shift of the accent] may express a consequent (logical and/or chronological) situation to a situation represented by a volitional form (cohortative, imperataive, jussive…)"; they translate our clause (§32.2.2b): "Let me glean *and* (*so*) gather." Cf. Lambdin §107b, who states that this construction expresses explicit consecution: do *x* and then *y* and then *z*. So also Joüon §§119j, 122c and GKC §112q. See also Seow, p. 243, and Berg 2 §10q.
בָעֳמָרִים	n, m, pl, abs עֹמֶר √עמר w/ def art and prep בְּ "among the sheaves"
אַחֲרֵי	prep "behind, after" (properly n, m, pl, cs אַחַר √אחר "hinder parts of")
הַקּוֹצְרִים	v, G, act, ptc, m, pl, abs √קצר w/ def art "the harvesters"
וַתָּבוֹא	v, G, impf, indic, 3, f, s √בוא w/ ו cons "and she came"
וַתַּעֲמוֹד	v, G, impf, indic, 3, f, s √עמד w/ ו cons "and she stood" The form with ו is deviant (BL §49v).

מֵאָז	adv אָז w/ prep מִן "from then" On מִן indicating the starting point of an action, see Brock §111e.
הַבֹּקֶר	n, m, s, abs בֹּקֶר √בקר w/ def art "the morning"
וְעַד־	prep עַד √עדה w/ ו conj "and until"
עַתָּה	temp adv עַתָּה √ענה "now"
זֶה	dem pron, prox, m, s זֶה "this"
שִׁבְתָּהּ	v, G, inf, cs √ישׁב w/ 3, f, s, gen sx "her sitting"
or	
	n, m, s, *st. pr.* שֶׁבֶת √שבת w/ 3, f, s, gen sx "her break"
הַבָּיִת	n, m, s, abs בַּיִת w/ def art "the house" functioning as prep "inside"
מְעָט	n, m, s, abs מְעָט √מעט "a little, a few"

2:8 וַיֹּאמֶר בֹּעַז אֶל־רוּת הֲלוֹא שָׁמַעַתְּ בִּתִּי אַל־תֵּלְכִי לִלְקֹט בְּשָׂדֶה אַחֵר וְגַם לֹא תַעֲבוּרִי מִזֶּה וְכֹה תִדְבָּקִין עִם־נַעֲרֹתָי:

2:8 Boaz said to Ruth, "Are you not listening, my daughter? Do not go glean in another field, do not even leave here; rather, stick closely to my young women."

וַיֹּאמֶר	v, G, impf, indic, 3, m, s √אמר w/ ו cons "and he said"
בֹּעַז	PN "Boaz"
אֶל־	prep אֶל "to"
רוּת	PN "Ruth"
הֲלוֹא שָׁמַעַתְּ	v, G, pf, 2, f, s √שמע w/ neg part לֹא and interr ה "are you not listening?" On the translation of stative verbs in the suffix conjugation with a present tense, see Joüon §112a.
בִּתִּי	n, f, s, *st. pr.* בַּת √בנה? w/ 1, c, s, gen sx "my daughter"
אַל־תֵּלְכִי	v, G, impf, juss, 2, f, s √הלך w/ neg part אַל "don't walk, go"
לִלְקֹט	v, G, inf, cs √לקט w/ prep לְ "to glean" The לְ expresses a weakly nuanced finality (i.e., purpose or result); see Joüon §168c.

בְּשָׂדֶה	n, m, s, abs שָׂדֶה √שדה w/ prep בְּ "in a field"
אַחֵר	adj, m, s, abs אַחֵר √אחר "another"
וְגַם	adv גַּם √גמם w/ וּ conj "and also"
לֹא תַעֲבוּרִי	v, G, impf, indic, 2, f, s √עבר w/ neg part אַל "don't leave" This is an abnormal or faulty form (Joüon §44c, BL §49v, GKC §47g). Berg 2 §14g says that the plene spelling is a pausal form with an incorrect *û* for *ō*.
מִזֶּה	dem pron, prox, m, s זֶה w/ prep מִן "from this one"
וְכֹה	dem adv כֹּה w/ וּ disj "but thus [≈ rather]" On כֹּה here, see *IBHS* §31.7.1 n. 51.
תִדְבָּקִין	v, G, impf, indic, 2, f, s √דבק w/ paragogic *nûn* "stick closely" On paragogic *nûn* ("stuck-on *nûn*"), see *IBHS* §31.7.1a, Joüon §44f, BL §40q, GKC §47o. On the pretonic lengthening instead of the expected reduction, see Berg 2 §5a.
עִם־נַעֲרֹתַי	n, f, pl, *st. pr.* נַעֲרָה √נער w/ 1, c, s, gen sx and prep עִם √עמם "with my young women"

2:9 עֵינַ֜יִךְ בַּשָּׂדֶ֣ה אֲשֶׁר־יִקְצֹרוּן֮ וְהָלַ֣כְתְּ אַחֲרֵיהֶן֒ הֲל֥וֹא צִוִּ֛יתִי אֶת־הַנְּעָרִ֖ים לְבִלְתִּ֣י נָגְעֵ֑ךְ וְצָמִ֗ת וְהָלַכְתְּ֙ אֶל־הַכֵּלִ֔ים וְשָׁתִ֕ית מֵאֲשֶׁ֥ר יִשְׁאֲב֖וּן הַנְּעָרִֽים׃

2:9   "Let your eyes be on the field in which they reap and walk after them. Have I not commanded the young men not to touch you? If you thirst, go to the vessels and drink from that which the young men shall draw."

עֵינַיִךְ	n, f, du, cs עַיִן √עין w/ 2, f, s, gen sx "your eyes"
בַּשָּׂדֶה	n, m, s, abs שָׂדֶה √שדה w/ def art and prep בְּ "on the field"
אֲשֶׁר־	rel pron אֲשֶׁר √אשר "that"
יִקְצֹרוּן	v, G, impf, indic, 3, m, pl √קצר w/ paragogic *nûn* "they will harvest" On paragogic *nûn* here, see Joüon §44e, BL §40q, and GKC §47m. According to Berg 2 §5b, instead of pretonic reduction with the paragogic *nûn*, there is pretoninc lengthening (the *ḥōlem* of our word) nearly always with heavy disjunction, often with light disjunction (the situation here), and sporadically with conjunctive accents.

וְהָלַכְתְּ   v, G, pf, 3, f, s √הלך w/ ו cons "and you will walk"

אַחֲרֵיהֶן   prep "behind, after" (properly n, m, pl, cs אַחַר √אחר "hinder parts of") w/ 3, f, pl, gen sx "after them"

הֲלוֹא צִוִּיתִי   v, D, pf, 1, c, s √צוה w/ neg part לֹא and interr ה "have I not commanded?"
The *qatal* form is used sometimes for an action that will appear in reality in the future (see Joüon §112g). GKC §106m states that the perfect is used to "express *future* actions, when the speaker intends ... to represent them as finished, or as equivalent to accomplished facts ... [in] contracts or other express stipulations." In our passage the sense is "I hereby command. . . ."

אֶת־הַנְּעָרִים   n, m, pl, abs נַעַר √נער w/ def art and sign def dir obj "the young men"

לְבִלְתִּי   neg part בִּלְתִּי (from בֶּלֶת [בלה√?]; cf. Ugaritic *blt*) w/ לְ used to negate infinitives "not to..."

נׇגְעֵךְ   v, G, inf, cs √נגע w/ 2, f, s, acc sx "to touch you"
The root נגע with the accusative is rare; usually there is an intervening preposition (Joüon §125b). BL §52h calls this a neoformation according to the strong verb.

וְצָמִת   v, G, pf, 2, f, s √צמא w/ ו cons "and if you should thirst" = "whenever you thirst"
The perfect may introduce a protasis; see GKC §§112kk, 159g. On the form, see Joüon §78g, BL §54r, GKC §75qq, and Berg 2 §29e.

וְהָלַכְתְּ   v, G, pf, 2, f, s √הלך w/ ו cons "then you should go"
The perfect consecutive may introduce the apodosis after a perfect in the protasis (GKC §§112kk, 159g). Joüon §§166b, 167b, however, sees this sentence not as a conditional but as a temporal construction: "when you thirst, you will go." Remember that the *wāw* consecutive attached to the perfect is not morphologically marked. However, first common singular and second masculine singular perfect consecutives will have the accent shifted to the end of the word, a condition that does not apply here, since this form is a second *feminine* singular.

אֶל־הַכֵּלִים   n, m, pl, abs כְּלִי √כלה w/ def art and prep אֶל "to the vessels"

וְשָׁתִית   v, G, pf, 2, f, s √שתה w/ ו cons "and drink"

מֵאֲשֶׁר   rel pron אֲשֶׁר √אשר w/ prep מִן "from that which"

יִשְׁאֲבוּן   v, G, impf, indic, 3, m, pl √שאב w/ paragogic *nûn* "they shall draw"
On paragogic *nûn* here, see Joüon §44e, BL §40q, and GKC §47m.

הַנְּעָרִים   n, m, pl, abs נַעַר √נער w/ def art "the young men"

34

2:10 וַתִּפֹּל עַל־פָּנֶיהָ וַתִּשְׁתַּחוּ אָרְצָה וַתֹּאמֶר אֵלָיו מַדּוּעַ מָצָאתִי חֵן בְּעֵינֶיךָ לְהַכִּירֵנִי וְאָנֹכִי נָכְרִיָּה:

2:10 She fell on her face, bowed to the ground, and said to him, "Why have I found favor in your eyes to the point of noticing me? I am a foreigner!"

וַתִּפֹּל	v, G, impf, indic, 3, f, s √נפל w/ וֹ cons "and she fell"
עַל־	prep עַל √עלה "on"
פָּנֶיהָ	n, m, pl, *st. pr.* פָּנֶה √פנה w/ 3, f, s, gen sx "her face"
וַתִּשְׁתַּחוּ	v, Št, impf, indic, 3, f, s √חוה w/ וֹ cons "and she bowed down"
אָרְצָה	n, f, s, *st. pr.* אֶרֶץ √ארץ w/ loc ה "to the ground"
וַתֹּאמֶר	v, G, impf, indic, 3, f, s √אמר w/ וֹ cons "and she said"
אֵלָיו	prep אֶל w/ 3, m, s, gen sx "to him"
מַדּוּעַ	interr adv מַדּוּעַ √ידע (probably contracted from מָה יוֹדֵעַ "what being known?") "wherefore? on what account? why? how?"
מָצָאתִי	v, G, pf, 1, c, s √מצא "I have found"
חֵן	n, m, s, abs חֵן √חנן "favor, grace"
בְּעֵינֶיךָ	n, f, du, *st. pr.* עַיִן √עין w/ 2, m, s, gen sx and w/ prep בְּ "in your eyes"
לְהַכִּירֵנִי	v, H, inf, cs √נכר w/ 1, c, s, acc sx and w/ prep לְ "to recognize, take note of me"

According to *IBHS* §36.2.3d, an infinitive construct with לְ can express result clauses, which "express a consequence of the main verb ('and so; so that')"; they translate our clause: "Why have I found such favor in your eyes *that* you *notice* me?" According to Jouön §124l, the infinitive construct with לְ here is the equivalent of an imperfect with a *wāw* consecutive: "that you are interested in me." Also, Jouön §124s states that the tense, aspect of action, and subject for an infinitive is indicated only by the context. According to Wms §198, an infinitive construct with לְ may be translated "so as to," to which understanding Berg 2 §57k adds: "often with consecutive secondary meaning" (here the infinitive adds to the מָצָאתִי חֵן). According to GKC §115c, the only verbal suffixes (as indicated by the נ) attached to the infinitive construct are the first common singular and plural; all other persons and numbers are attached to the sign of the definite direct object אֶת, or the genitive suffixes attached to nouns are used.

וְאָנֹכִ֖י	indep pers pron, 1, c, s אָנֹכִי w/ ו disj "but I"
נָכְרִיָּ֑ה	adj, f, s, abs נכר√ נָכְרִי "a foreigner"

2:11 וַיַּ֨עַן בֹּ֜עַז וַיֹּ֣אמֶר לָ֗הּ הֻגֵּ֨ד הֻגַּ֤ד לִי֙ כֹּ֣ל אֲשֶׁר־עָשִׂ֣ית אֶת־חֲמוֹתֵ֔ךְ אַחֲרֵ֖י מ֣וֹת אִישֵׁ֑ךְ וַתַּֽעַזְבִ֞י אָבִ֣יךְ וְאִמֵּ֗ךְ וְאֶ֙רֶץ֙ מֽוֹלַדְתֵּ֔ךְ וַתֵּ֣לְכִ֔י אֶל־עַ֕ם אֲשֶׁ֥ר לֹא־יָדַ֖עַתְּ תְּמ֥וֹל שִׁלְשֽׁוֹם:

2:11 Boaz answered and said to her "All that you did for your mother-in-law after the death of your husband has been fully related to me: you left your father, mother, and the land of your birth, and went to a people whom you had not known before."

וַיַּ֨עַן	v, G, impf, indic, 3, m, s ענה√ w/ ו cons "and he said"
בֹּ֜עַז	PN "Boaz"
וַיֹּ֣אמֶר	v, G, impf, indic, 3, m, s אמר√ w/ ו cons "and he said"
לָ֗הּ	prep לְ w/ 3, f, s, gen sx "to her"
הֻגֵּ֨ד	v, Hp, inf, abs נגד√ "to be told, announced" On the significance of an infinitive absolute with a perfect verb, see Berg 2 §12e.
הֻגַּ֤ד	v, Hp, pf, 3, m, s נגד√ "it was told"
לִי֙	prep לְ w/ 1, c, s, gen sx "to me"
כֹּ֣ל	n, m, s, abs כלל√ כֹּל "all" BL §6m states that, according to the Talmud, there are seven cases in which something is not written but still read: פְּרָת 2 Sam 8:3; אִישׁ 2 Sam 16:23; בָּאִים Jer 31:38; לָהּ Jer 50:29; [כֹּל] אֵת Ruth 2:11; אֵלַי Ruth 3:5, 17. Conversely, there are five cases in which words present in the text are not read: נָא 2 Kgs 5:18; וְאֵת Jer 32:11; ידרך Jer 51:3; חֲמֵשׁ Ezek 48:16; אִם Ruth 3:12.
אֲשֶׁר־	rel pron אֲשֶׁר אשר√ "that"
עָשִׂ֣ית	v, G, pf, 2, f, s עשה√ "you did"
אֶת־	prep אֵת "with"
חֲמוֹתֵ֔ךְ	n, f, s, *st. pr.* חָמוֹת חמה√ w/ 2, f, s, gen sx "your mother-in-law"
אַחֲרֵ֖י	prep "behind, after" (properly n, m, pl, cs אַחַר אחר√ "hinder parts of")
מ֣וֹת	n, m, s, cs מָוֶת מות√ "the death of"

אִישֵׁךְ	n, m, s, *st. pr.* אִישׁ w/ 2, f, s, gen sx "your husband"
וַתַּעַזְבִי	v, G, impf, indic, 2, f, s √עזב w/ ו cons "and you left"
אָבִיךְ	n, m, s, *st. pr.* אָב √אבה w/ 2, f, s, gen sx "your father"
וְאִמֵּךְ	n, f, s, *st. pr.* אֵם √אמם w/ 2, f, s, gen sx and w/ ו conj "and your mother"
וְאֶרֶץ	n, f, s, cs אֶרֶץ √ארץ w/ ו conj "and the land of"
מוֹלַדְתֵּךְ	v, H, ptc, f, s, *st. pr.* √ילד w/ 2, f, s, gen sx "your birthing, kindred, birth, offspring"
וַתֵּלְכִי	v, G, impf, indic, 2, f, s √הלך w/ ו cons "and you walked"
אֶל־	prep אֶל "to"
עַם	n, m, s, abs עַם √עמם "a people"
אֲשֶׁר	rel pron אֲשֶׁר √אשר "that" The relative pronoun may occur after either a definite or indefinite noun (Joüon §158f).
לֹא־	neg part לֹא
יָדַעַתְּ	v, G, pf, 2, f, s √ידע "you did not know"
תְּמוֹל	n, m, s, cs תְּמוֹל functioning as temp adv "yesterday"
שִׁלְשׁוֹם	temp adv "three days ago" שִׁלְשֹׁם √שלש The phrase תְּמוֹל שִׁלְשֹׁם means "yesterday (and) day before," which is idiomatic for "hitherto." The phrase modifies לֹא־יָדַעַתְּ, not וַתֵּלְכִי.

2:12 יְשַׁלֵּם יְהוָה פָּעֳלֵךְ וּתְהִי מַשְׂכֻּרְתֵּךְ שְׁלֵמָה מֵעִם יְהוָה אֱלֹהֵי יִשְׂרָאֵל אֲשֶׁר־בָּאת לַחֲסוֹת תַּחַת־כְּנָפָיו:

2:12 "May YHWH repay your work, and may your wage be complete from YHWH, the God of Israel, under whose wings you have come to seek refuge."

יְשַׁלֵּם	v, D, impf, juss, 3, m, s √שלם "may he repay"
יְהוָה	DN "YHWH"
פָּעֳלֵךְ	n, m, s, *st. pr.* פֹּעַל √פעל w/ 2, f, s, gen sx "your deed, work"
וּתְהִי	v, G, impf, juss, 3, f, s √היה w/ ו conj "and may it be"

מַשְׂכֻּרְתֵּ֑ךְ	n, f, s, *st. pr.* מַשְׂכֹּרֶת √שכר w/ 2, f, s, gen sx "your wage"
שְׁלֵמָ֑ה	adj, f, s, abs שָׁלֵם √שלם "complete, safe, at peace"
מֵעִ֣ם	prep עִם √עמם "with" w/ prep מִן "from" = "from with; from"
יְהוָ֗ה	DN "YHWH"
אֱלֹהֵ֣י	n, m, s, cs אֱלֹהִים √אלה "the God of"
יִשְׂרָאֵ֔ל	GN "Israel"
אֲשֶׁר־	rel pron אֲשֶׁר √אשר "whose"
בָּ֖את	v, G, pf, 2, f, s √בוא "you came"
לַחֲס֥וֹת	v, G, inf, cs √חסה w/ prep לְ "to seek refuge" An unusual form וְלַחְסוֹת occurs in Isa 30:2 (Joüon §68e). On the form, see Berg 2 §21i.
תַּֽחַת־	n, m, s, cs תַּחַת √תחת functioning as a prep "under"
כְּנָפָֽיו	n, f, du, *st. pr.* כָּנָף √כנף w/ 3, m, s, gen sx "his wings"

2:13 וַתֹּ֡אמֶר אֶמְצָא־חֵן֩ בְּעֵינֶ֨יךָ אֲדֹנִ֜י כִּ֣י נִֽחַמְתָּ֗נִי וְכִ֤י דִבַּ֙רְתָּ֙ עַל־לֵ֣ב שִׁפְחָתֶ֔ךָ וְאָנֹכִ֕י לֹ֥א אֶֽהְיֶ֖ה כְּאַחַ֥ת שִׁפְחֹתֶֽיךָ׃

2:13 She said, "May I continue to find favor in your eyes, my lord, since you have comforted me, and since you have spoken to the heart of your maidservant, even though I am not even like one of your maidservants."

וַתֹּ֡אמֶר	v, G, impf, indic, 3, f, s √אמר w/ וּ cons "and she said"
אֶמְצָא־	v, G, impf, indic, 1, c, s √מצא "may I find" According to Berg 2 §10o, the simple imperfect here has the sense of the cohortative.
חֵן	n, m, s, abs חֵן √חנן "favor"
בְּעֵינֶ֨יךָ	n, f, du, *st. pr.* עַיִן w/ 2, m, s, gen sx and w/ prep בְּ "in your eyes"
אֲדֹנִ֜י	n, m, s, *st. pr.* אָדוֹן √אדן w/ 1, c, s, gen sx "my lord"
כִּי	conj כִּי "since"
נִֽחַמְתָּ֗נִי	v, D, pf, 2, m, s √נחם w/ 1, c, s, acc sx "you have comforted me"

So BDB and *HALOT* (*s.v.* √נחם). The *ḥêt* is virtually doubled. Though the form could be parsed as an N perfect, the accusative suffix and the context require the D.

וְכִי — conj כִּי w/ ו conj "and since"

דִּבַּ֫רְתָּ — v, D, pf, 2, m, s √דבר "you have spoken"

עַל־ — prep עַל √עלה "on"

לֵב — n, m, s, cs לֵב √לבב "the heart of"

שִׁפְחָתֶ֫ךָ — n, f, s, cs שִׁפְחָה √שׁפח w/ 2, m, s, gen sx "your maidservant"

וְאָנֹכִי — indep pers pron, 1, c, s אָנֹכִי w/ ו disj "but I"

לֹא אֶהְיֶה — v, G, impf, indic, 1, c, s √היה w/ neg part לֹא "I am not"

כְּאַחַת — card, f, s, cs אַחַד √אחד w/ prep כְּ "like one of"
IBHS §15.2.1f: "The substantive uses of אַחַד / אַחַת chiefly involve construct phrases."

שִׁפְחֹתֶ֫יךָ — n, f, pl, *st. pr.* שִׁפְחָה √שׁפח w/ 2, m, s, gen sx "your maidservants"

2:14 וַיֹּ֩אמֶר֩ לָ֨ה בֹ֜עַז לְעֵ֣ת הָאֹ֗כֶל גֹּ֤שִֽׁי הֲלֹם֙ וְאָכַ֣לְתְּ מִן־הַלֶּ֔חֶם וְטָבַ֥לְתְּ פִּתֵּ֖ךְ בַּחֹ֑מֶץ וַתֵּ֨שֶׁב֙ מִצַּ֣ד הַקּֽוֹצְרִ֔ים וַיִּצְבָּט־לָ֣הּ קָלִ֔י וַתֹּ֥אכַל וַתִּשְׂבַּ֖ע וַתֹּתַֽר׃

2:14 Boaz said to her at meal time, "Come here and eat some of the food and dip your part in the vinegar." She sat beside the harvesters, and he held out parched grain to her; she ate until she was sated and even left some.

וַיֹּ֩אמֶר֩ — v, G, impf, indic, 3, m, s √אמר w/ ו cons "and he said"

לָ֨ה — prep לְ w/ 3, f, s, gen sx "to her"
On the unexpected ה instead of the expected הּ, see BL §81f′, GKC §103g, and Joüon §§25a, 103f. See also Berg 1 §16e.

בֹּ֜עַז — PN "Boaz"

לְעֵ֣ת — n, m, s, cs עֵת √ענה w/ prep לְ "to the time of"
On the accent, see Berg 1 §22f.

הָאֹ֗כֶל — n, m, s, abs אֹכֶל √אכל w/ def art "the food"
The accentuation requires the quote to begin after this word and not after בֹּ֫עַז (Joüon §15k).

גְּשִׁי   v, G, impf, impv, 2, f, s √נגש "draw near!"
The imperative can have the force of invitation; so *BHRG* §19.4.2 (i) d. *IBHS* 34.4a: "The positive imperative differs from the regulative or legislative non-perfective in being more urgent or in demanding immediate, specific action on the part of the adressee." Joüon §114m: "The imperative is employed above all for an immediate action." GKC §66c calls this form "curious," and BL §52t lists it as deviating. See also Berg 2 §25c.

הֲלֹם   loc adv הֲלֹם "hither"

וְאָכַלְתְּ   v, G, pf, 2, f, s, √אכל w/ ו cons "and eat!"
The perfect consecutive is common after the imperative of verbs of motion (so Joüon §119l n. 1). See further Lambdin §107b, where he states that a perfect after an imperative indicates explicit consecution: do *x* and then *y* and then *z*.

מִן־   prep מִן "from"

הַלֶּחֶם   n, m, s, abs לֶחֶם √לחם w/ def art "the bread"

וְטָבַלְתְּ   v, G, pf, 2, f, s √טבל w/ ו cons "dip"

פִּתֵּךְ   n, f, s, *st. pr.* פַּת √פתת w/ 2, f, s, gen sx "your morsel, portion"

בַּחֹמֶץ   n, m, s, abs חֹמֶץ √חמץ w/ def art and w/ prep בְּ "in the vinegar"

וַתֵּשֶׁב   v, G, impf, indic, 3, f, s √ישב w/ ו cons "and she sat"

מִצַּד   n, m, s, cs צַד √צדד w/ prep מִן "from the side of"

הַקּוֹצְרִים   v, G, act, ptc, m, pl, abs √קצר w/ def art "the harvesters"
The active participle has four functions in Biblical Hebrew: as a substantive (as here), an adjective, a relative (i.e., the participle modifies an antecedent substantive), and a predicate (see *IBHS* 37.1c).

וַיִּצְבָּט־   v, G, impf, indic, 3, m, s √צבט w/ ו cons "and he held out"

לָהּ   prep לְ w/ 3, f, s, gen sx "to her"

קָלִי   n, m, s, abs קָלִי √קלה "parched grain"

וַתֹּאכַל   v, G, impf, indic, 3, f, s √אכל w/ ו cons "and she ate"

וַתִּשְׂבַּע   v, G, impf, indic, 3, f, s √שבע w/ ו cons "and she was sated"

וַתֹּתַר   v, H, impf, indic, 3, f, s √יתר w/ ו cons "and she left some"
According to GKC §53n, the shortened form of the H is due to the *wāw* consecutive, and the *a* is due to the principal pause and the ר (GKC §69v); so also Berg 2 §23e and 2 §26h. On the missing pausal form, see BL §46aʹ.

2:15 וַתָּ֙קָם֙ לְלַקֵּ֔ט וַיְצַו֩ בֹּ֨עַז אֶת־נְעָרָ֜יו לֵאמֹ֗ר גַּ֣ם בֵּ֧ין הָעֳמָרִ֛ים תְּלַקֵּ֖ט וְלֹ֥א תַכְלִימֽוּהָ׃

2:15 She got up to glean, and Boaz commanded his young men saying, "Let her glean even between the sheaves, and do not hassle her!"

וַתָּ֙קָם֙	v, G, impf, indic, 3, f, s √קום w/ ו cons "and she arose"
לְלַקֵּט	v, D, inf, cs √לקט w/ prep לְ "to glean"
וַיְצַו֩	v, G, impf, indic, 3, m, s √צוה w/ ו cons "and he commanded"
בֹּ֨עַז	PN "Boaz" On the unexpected *dagesh lene* after a diphthong, see Berg 1 §18e.
אֶת־נְעָרָיו	n, m, pl, *st. pr.* נַעַר√נער w/ 3, m, s, gen sx and sign def dir obj "his young men"
לֵאמֹר	v, G, inf, cs √אמר w/ prep לְ "saying"
גַּם	adv גַּם √גמם "also, moreover, yea"
בֵּין	subs cs בַּ֫יִן "interval, space between," always as prep בֵּין √בין "between"
הָעֳמָרִים	n, m, pl, abs עֹ֫מֶר √עמר w/ def art "the sheaves" The article is הָ before עֳ (GKC §35k).
תְּלַקֵּט	v, D, impf, juss, 3, f, s √לקט "let her glean" Joüon §113l understands this form not as a jussive but as an indicative with a nuance of *be able, be allowed to:* "she will be able to glean."
וְלֹא תַכְלִימֽוּהָ	v, H, impf, indic, 2, m, pl √כלם w/ 3, f, s, acc sx and neg part לֹא w/ ו conj "and never harass, hassle, or humiliate her"

2:16 וְגַ֛ם שֹׁל־תָּשֹׁ֥לּוּ לָ֖הּ מִן־הַצְּבָתִ֑ים וַעֲזַבְתֶּ֛ם וְלִקְּטָ֖ה וְלֹ֥א תִגְעֲרוּ־בָֽהּ׃

2:16 "Also you shall by all means pull out for her some from the bundles and leave so that she may glean, and do not rebuke her!"

וְגַם	adv גַּם √גמם w/ ו conj "and also, moreover, yea"
שֹׁל־	v, G, inf, abs √שלל "drawing out" On the form of ע״ע infinitive absolutes, see BL §58p′ and GKC §67o. According to Joüon §123q, "instead of the infinitive absolute, Qal, sometimes there is the form of the infinitive construct: In the verbs: ע״ע … שֹׁל for שָׁלוֹל Ruth 2:16 (but the text is probably altered; compare infinitive construct שְׁלֹל §82k)"; Berg 2

§12f and GKC §113x agree that sometimes an infinitive construct substitutes for an infinitive absolute, but Berg 2 §27a* recognizes that there is debate as to whether this form is an infinitive absolute or an infinitive construct. The cognate infinitive serves to emphasize the verb itself, according to Berg 2 §12c.

תָּשֹׁלּוּ   v, G, impf, indic, 2, m, pl √שלל "you shall draw out"

לָהּ   prep לְ w/ 3, f, s, gen sx "for her"

מִן־הַצְּבָתִים   n, m, *pl. tan.*, abs צְבָתִים √צבת w/ def art and prep מִן "from the bundles"

וַעֲזַבְתֶּם   v, G, pf, 2, m, pl √עזב w/ ו cons "and you will leave"

וְלִקְּטָה   v, D, pf, 3, f, s √לקט w/ ו cons "and she will glean"

וְלֹא־תִגְעֲרוּ־   v, G, impf, indic, 2, m, pl √גער w/ neg part לֹא and ו conj "and you will not rebuke"

בָהּ   prep בְּ w/ 3, f, s, gen sx "against her"

2:17 וַתְּלַקֵּט בַּשָּׂדֶה עַד־הָעָרֶב וַתַּחְבֹּט אֵת אֲשֶׁר־לִקֵּטָה וַיְהִי כְּאֵיפָה שְׂעֹרִים:

2:17   She gleaned in the field until evening and then threshed that which she had gleaned, which was about an ephah of barley.

וַתְּלַקֵּט   v, D, impf, indic, 3, f, s √לקט w/ ו cons "and she gleaned"

בַּשָּׂדֶה   n, m, s, abs שָׂדֶה √שדה w/ def art and w/ prep בְּ "in the field"

עַד־   prep עַד √עדה "until"

הָעָרֶב   n, m, s, abs עֶרֶב √ערב w/ def art "the evening"

וַתַּחְבֹּט   v, G, impf, indic, 3, f, s √חבט w/ ו cons "and she threshed"

אֵת אֲשֶׁר־   rel pron אֲשֶׁר √אשר w/ sign def dir obj "that which"

לִקֵּטָה   v, G, pf, 3, f, s √לקט "she gleaned"

וַיְהִי   v, G, impf, indic, 3, m, s √היה w/ ו cons "and it was"

כְּאֵיפָה   n, f, s, abs אֵיפָה √אפה w/ prep כְּ "about an ephah"
On כְּ meaning "about," see Joüon §133g and Brock §109a; on the omission of אֶחָד but still retaining the sense of "one," see Joüon §137u n. 1.

שְׂעֹרִים   n, f, pl, abs שְׂעֹרָה √שער "barley"
Note that שְׂעֹרִים is in apposition to כְּאֵיפָה, giving a meaning of "about a barley ephah" = "about an ephah of barley" (*IBHS* §12.3d n. 9).

2:18 וַתִּשָּׂא֙ וַתָּב֣וֹא הָעִ֔יר וַתֵּ֥רֶא חֲמוֹתָ֖הּ אֵ֣ת אֲשֶׁר־לִקֵּ֑טָה וַתּוֹצֵא֙ וַתִּתֶּן־לָ֔הּ אֵ֥ת אֲשֶׁר־הוֹתִ֖רָה מִשָּׂבְעָֽהּ׃

2:18   She lifted it up and entered the city, and her mother-in-law saw that which she had gleaned. She brought out that which she had saved from her abundance and gave it to her.

וַתִּשָּׂא֙	v, G, impf, indic, 3, f, s √נשא w/ ו cons "and she lifted up"
וַתָּב֣וֹא	v, G, impf, indic, 3, f, s √בוא w/ ו cons "and she came"
הָעִ֔יר	n, f, s, abs √עיר w/ def art "the city"
וַתֵּ֥רֶא	v, G, impf, indic, 3, f, s √ראה w/ ו cons "and she saw"
חֲמוֹתָ֖הּ	n, f, s, *st. pr.* √חמה חָמוֹת w/ 3, f, s, gen sx, "her mother-in-law"
אֵ֣ת אֲשֶׁר־	rel pron אֲשֶׁר √אשר and sign def dir obj "that which"
לִקֵּ֑טָה	v, D, pf, 3, f, s √לקט "she gleaned"
וַתּוֹצֵא֙	v, H, impf, indic, 3, f, s √יצא w/ ו cons "and she brought out"
וַתִּתֶּן־לָ֔הּ	v, G, impf, indic, 3, f, s √נתן w/ prep לְ and 3, f, s, gen sx and ו cons "and she gave to her"
אֵ֥ת אֲשֶׁר־	rel pron אֲשֶׁר √אשר and sign def dir obj "that which"
הוֹתִ֖רָה	v, H, pf, 3, f, s √יתר "she left"
מִשָּׂבְעָֽהּ	n, m, s, *st. pr.* √שבע w/ 3, f, s, gen sx and prep מִן "from her satiety, abundance"

2:19 וַתֹּאמֶר֩ לָ֨הּ חֲמוֹתָ֜הּ אֵיפֹ֨ה לִקַּ֤טְתְּ הַיּוֹם֙ וְאָ֣נָה עָשִׂ֔ית יְהִ֥י מַכִּירֵ֖ךְ בָּר֑וּךְ וַתַּגֵּ֣ד לַחֲמוֹתָ֗הּ אֵ֤ת אֲשֶׁר־עָשְׂתָה֙ עִמּ֔וֹ וַתֹּ֗אמֶר שֵׁ֤ם הָאִישׁ֙ אֲשֶׁ֨ר עָשִׂ֧יתִי עִמּ֛וֹ הַיּ֖וֹם בֹּֽעַז׃

2:19   Her mother-in-law said to her, "Where did you glean today, and where did you work? May he who noticed you be blessed!" She reported to her mother-in-law with whom she had worked and said, "The name of the man with whom I worked today is Boaz."

וַתֹּאמֶר֩	v, G, impf, indic, 3, f, s √אמר w/ ו cons "and she said"
לָ֨הּ	prep לְ w/ 3, f, s, gen sx "to her"

חֲמוֹתָהּ   n, f, s, *st. pr.* חָמוֹת √חמה w/ 3, f, s, gen sx, "her mother-in-law"

אֵיפֹה   adv (אֵי "where?" + פֹּה "here") "where?"
On the uses of אֵיפֹה, see *BHRG* §43.3.7. *IBHS* §18.4a explains, "An elaborate network of interrogative terms is organized around אֵי 'where?'…. Most of these terms are locative in reference and strictly interrogative in use."

לִקַּטְתְּ   v, D, pf, 2, f, s √לקט "you gleaned"

הַיּוֹם   n, m, s, abs יוֹם w/ def art "today"

וְאָנָה   adv אָן (contracted from אַיִן) w/ loc ה and ו conj "and where," or "and to where?"
IBHS §18.4f: "אָנָה [is] apparently אָן with the directional *h*." According to *BHRG* §43.3.8 (ii), "In exceptional cases אָנָה is used to enquire about the place *in which* an event occurred: *where?*"

עָשִׂית   v, G, pf, 2, f, s √עשה "you worked"

יְהִי   v, G, impf, juss, 3, m, s √היה "may he be"

מַכִּירֵךְ   v, H, ptc, m, s, *st. pr.* √נכר w/ 2, f, s, acc sx "he who noticed you"

בָּרוּךְ   v, G, pass, ptc, m, s, abs √ברך "blessed"
IBHS §37.7.1a: "The verb היה serves as an independent verb with participles used as substantives … or adjectives…, including all passive participles"; so also Berg 2 §13l.

וַתַּגֵּד   v, H, impf, 3, f, s √נגד w/ ו cons "and she reported, declared"

לַחֲמוֹתָהּ   n, f, s, *st. pr.* חָמוֹת √חמה w/ 3, f, s, gen sx and prep לְ "to her mother-in-law"

אֶת אֲשֶׁר־   rel pron אֲשֶׁר √אשר and sign def dir obj "him who"

עָשְׂתָה עִמּוֹ   v, G, pf, 3, f, s √עשה w/ prep עִם √עממ and 3, m, s, gen sx "she worked with him"

וַתֹּאמֶר   v, G, impf, indic, 3, f, s √אמר w/ ו cons "and she said"

שֵׁם   n, m, s, cs שֵׁם "the name of"

הָאִישׁ   n, m, s, abs אִישׁ √אנשׁ? w/ def art "the man"

אֲשֶׁר   rel pron אֲשֶׁר √אשר "him who"

עָשִׂיתִי עִמּוֹ   v, G, pf, 1, c, s √עשה w/ prep עִם √עממ and 3, m, s, gen sx and rel pron אֲשֶׁר √אשר "I worked with him"

הַיּוֹם   n, m, s, abs יוֹם w/ def art "today"

בֹּעַז   PN "Boaz"

2:20 וַתֹּאמֶר נָעֳמִי לְכַלָּתָהּ בָּרוּךְ הוּא לַיהוָה אֲשֶׁר לֹא־עָזַב חַסְדּוֹ אֶת־הַחַיִּים וְאֶת־הַמֵּתִים וַתֹּאמֶר לָהּ נָעֳמִי קָרוֹב לָנוּ הָאִישׁ מִגֹּאֲלֵנוּ הוּא:

2:20   Naomi said to her daughter-in-law, "Blessed be he to YHWH, who has not withheld his covenant-loyalty from the living and the dead." Naomi said to her, "The man is our relative; he is one of our kinsman-redeemers."

וַתֹּאמֶר	v, G, impf, indic, 3, f, s אמר√ w/ ו cons "and she said"
נָעֳמִי	PN "Naomi"
לְכַלָּתָהּ	n, f, s, *st. pr.* כַּלָּה כלל√ w/ 3, f, s, gen sx and prep לְ "to her daughter-in-law"
בָּרוּךְ	v, G, pass, ptc, m, s ברך√ "blessed"
הוּא	indep pers pron, 3, m, s הוּא "he"
לַיהוָה	DN "YHWH" w/ prep לְ "to YHWH"
	IBHS §11.2.10d state, "The so-called indirect object of verbs of giving and some verbs of speaking and listening takes *l*," and remark in n. 72 on the לְ in our word, "Not 'by.' See Pardee, *UF* 8: 221–23, cf. 230; 9: 209." Contrast this with the position of GKC §121f: "The efficient cause (or personal agent) is, as a rule, attached to the passive by לְ (thus corresponding to the Greek and Latin dative), e.g. … the blessing בָּרוּךְ הוּא לַיהוָה *blessed be he of* [= by] *the Lord*" (Ruth 2:20; so also Joüon §132f).
אֲשֶׁר	rel pron אֲשֶׁר אשר√ "who"
לֹא־עָזַב	v, G, pf, 3, m, s עזב√ w/ neg part לֹא "he has not left, forsaken, loosed"
חַסְדּוֹ	n, m, s, *st. pr.* חֶסֶד חסד√ w/ 3, m, s, gen sx "his covenant-loyalty"
אֶת־הַחַיִּים	adj, m, pl, abs חַי חיה√ w/ def art and prep אֶת "with the living"
וְאֶת־הַמֵּתִים	v, G, act, ptc, m, pl מות√ w/ def art and prep אֶת and ו conj "and with the dead"
וַתֹּאמֶר	v, G, impf, indic, 3, f, s אמר√ w/ ו cons "and she said"
לָהּ	prep לְ w/ 3, f, s, gen sx "to her"
נָעֳמִי	PN "Naomi"
קָרוֹב	adj, m, s, abs קָרוֹב קרב√ "near"
לָנוּ	prep לְ w/ 1, c, pl, gen sx "to us, our"
הָאִישׁ	n, m, s, abs אִישׁ אנש√? w/ def art "the man"

מִגֹּאֲלֵנוּ — v, G, act, ptc, m, s (but read מִגֹּאֲלֵינוּ, i.e., pl), *st. pr.* √גאל w/ 1, c, pl, gen sx and prep מִן "one of our kinsman-redeemers"

הוּא — indep pers pron, 3, m, s הוּא "he"

2:21 וַתֹּאמֶר רוּת הַמּוֹאֲבִיָּה גַּם ׀ כִּי־אָמַר אֵלַי עִם־הַנְּעָרִים אֲשֶׁר־לִי תִּדְבָּקִין עַד אִם־כִּלּוּ אֵת כָּל־הַקָּצִיר אֲשֶׁר־לִי:

2:21 Ruth the Moabitess said, "Furthermore, he said to me, 'You should stick closely to my young people until they have finished the entire harvest that is mine.'"

וַתֹּאמֶר — v, G, impf, indic, 3, f, s √אמר w/ ו cons "and she said"

רוּת — PN "Ruth"

הַמּוֹאֲבִיָּה — gent adj, f, s, abs מוֹאֲבִיָּה (m, s מוֹאָבִי) w/ def art "the Moabitess"

גַּם ׀ כִּי־ — adv גַּם √גמם "also" w/ conj כִּי "that" = "even though" or "also, futhermore" Joüon §157a n. 2: "כִּי may introduce a subject clause after a simple אַף, גַּם, הֲ: ... Ruth 2:21 גַּם ׀ כִּי־אָמַר (there is) again (this) which he said = moreover, he said." On גַּם as "also," see Wms §378.

אָמַר — v, G, pf, 3, m, s √אמר "he said"

אֵלַי — prep אֶל w/ 1, c, s, gen sx "to me"

עִם־הַנְּעָרִים — n, m, pl, abs נַעַר √נער w/ def art and prep עִם √עמם "with the young people" Given the statement of 2:8 and the context here, נְעָרִים has "the sense of *young people* (of both genders)" (GKC §122g).

אֲשֶׁר־לִי — rel pron אֲשֶׁר √אשר w/ prep לְ and 1, c, s, gen sx "who are mine" GKC §135m n. 3: "Like the substantival genitive, according to §129h, the possessive pronoun may also be paraphrased by a relative clause, e.g. [Ruth 2:21] הַנְּעָרִים אֲשֶׁר לִי *the young men, which* are *to me*, i.e., *my young men*."

תִּדְבָּקִין — v, G, impf, indic, 2, f, s √דבק w/ paragogic *nûn* "stick closely" On paragogic *nûn* ("stuck-on *nûn*"), see *IBHS* §31.7.1a, Joüon §44f, BL §40q, GKC §47o.

עַד אִם־ — prep עַד √עדה "until" w/ hypoth part אִם "if" = "until which time" On this understanding of the phrase with the following perfect, see Joüon §112i and Wms §457.

כָּלּוּ   v, D, pf, 3, m, pl כלה√ "they finish"

אֶת כָּל־   n, m, s, cs כֹּל כלל√ w/ sign def dir obj "all of"

הַקָּצִיר   n, m, s, abs קָצִיר קצר√ w/ def art "the harvest"

אֲשֶׁר־לִי   rel pron אֲשֶׁר אשר√ w/ prep לְ and 1, c, s, gen sx, "that is mine"
                   According to Joüon §130e, the import of substituting אֲשֶׁר לְ for לְ is not clear.
                   Perhaps it is pointing out that Boaz only owns a portion of the harvest.

2:22 וַתֹּאמֶר נָעֳמִי אֶל־רוּת כַּלָּתָהּ טוֹב בִּתִּי כִּי תֵצְאִי עִם־נַעֲרוֹתָיו וְלֹא יִפְגְּעוּ־בָךְ בְּשָׂדֶה אַחֵר:

2:22 Naomi said to Ruth, her daughter-in-law, "It is good, my daughter, that you should go out with his young women and so not be harmed in another field."

וַתֹּאמֶר   v, G, impf, indic, 3, f, s אמר√ w/ וַ cons "and she said"

נָעֳמִי   PN "Naomi"

אֶל־רוּת   PN "Ruth" w/ prep אֶל "to Ruth"

כַּלָּתָהּ   n, f, s, *st. pr.* כַּלָּה כלל√ w/ 3, f, s, gen sx "her daughter-in-law"

טוֹב   adj, m, s, abs טוֹב טוב√ "good"
                   Joüon §141g understands this טוֹב as a comparative: "it is better, my daughter,
                   that you go with his girls than be harmed in another field."

בִּתִּי   n, f, s, *st. pr.* בַּת בנה√? w/ 1, c, s, gen sx "my daughter"

כִּי   conj כִּי "that"

תֵצְאִי   v, G, impf, indic, 2, f, s יצא√ "you should go out"
                   On this quasi-imperative sense of the imperfect with כִּי after a word such as
                   טוֹב (i.e., "it is better that…"), see Driver, p. 44.

עִם־נַעֲרוֹתָיו   n, f, pl, *st. pr.* נַעֲרָה נער√ w/ 3, m, s, gen sx and prep עִם עמם√ "with his young
                   women"

וְלֹא יִפְגְּעוּ־בָךְ   v, G, impf, indic, 3, m, pl פגע√ w/ prep בְּ and 2, f, s, gen sx "you" and neg part,
                   לֹא and וְ conj "that they will not assault you" = "that you will not be harmed"
                   An unspecified third masculine plural equals a passive, just as in English "they
                   say" equals "it is said." The context makes it clear that this is a purpose clause,
                   supporting the translation of the conjunction as "so that."

בְּשָׂדֶה	n, m, s, abs שָׂדֶה√שׂדה w/ prep בְּ "in a field"
אַחֵר	adj, m, s, abs אַחֵר√אחר "another"

2:23 וַתִּדְבַּק בְּנַעֲרוֹת בֹּעַז לְלַקֵּט עַד־כְּלוֹת קְצִיר־הַשְּׂעֹרִים וּקְצִיר הַחִטִּים וַתֵּשֶׁב אֶת־חֲמוֹתָהּ:

2:23   So Ruth clung to Boaz's young women to glean until the completion of the barley and wheat harvests, and she lived with her mother-in-law.

וַתִּדְבַּק	v, G, impf, indic, 3, f, s דבק√ w/ ו cons "and she clung"
בְּנַעֲרוֹת	n, f, pl, cs נַעֲרָה√נער w/ prep בְּ "to the young women of"
בֹּעַז	PN "Boaz"
לְלַקֵּט	v, D, inf, cs לקט√ w/ prep לְ "to glean"
עַד־כְּלוֹת	v, G, inf, cs כלה√ w/ prep עַד עדה√ "until the completion of"
קְצִיר־	n, m, s, cs קָצִיר√קצר "the harvest of"
הַשְּׂעֹרִים	n, f, pl, abs שְׂעֹרָה√שער w/ def art "the barley"
וּקְצִיר	n, m, s, cs קָצִיר√קצר w/ ו conj "and the harvest of"
הַחִטִּים	n, f, pl, abs חִטָּה√חנט w/ def art "the wheat"
וַתֵּשֶׁב	v, G, impf, indic, 3, f, s ישב√ w/ ו cons "and she lived"
אֶת־חֲמוֹתָהּ	n, f, s, *st. pr.* חָמוֹת√חמה w/ 3, f, s, gen sx and prep אֶת "with her mother-in-law"

48

RUTH 3:1–18

3:1 וַתֹּאמֶר לָהּ נָעֳמִי חֲמוֹתָהּ בִּתִּי הֲלֹא אֲבַקֶּשׁ־לָךְ מָנוֹחַ אֲשֶׁר יִיטַב־לָךְ:

3:1 Naomi, her mother-in-law, said to her, "My daughter, should I not seek security for you, so that all will be well with you?"

וַתֹּאמֶר	v, G, impf, indic, 3, f, s √אמר w/ ו cons "and she said"
לָהּ	prep לְ w/ 3, f, s, gen sx "to her"
נָעֳמִי	PN "Naomi"
חֲמוֹתָהּ	n, f, s, *st. pr.* חָמוֹת√חמה w/ 3, f, s, gen sx "her mother in law"
בִּתִּי	n, f, s, *st. pr.* בַּת √בנה? w/ 1, c, s, gen sx "my daughter"
הֲלֹא	neg part לֹא w/ interr ה "not? no?"
אֲבַקֶּשׁ־לָךְ	v, D, impf, indic, 1, c, s √בקשׁ w/ prep לְ w/ 2, f, s, gen sx "I should seek for you"
	According to Joüon §113m, the imperfect may have a nuance of obligation. According to *IBHS* §31.4e, "The *non-perfective* [i.e., imperfect] *of obligation* refers to either what the subject considers to be the subject's obligatory or necessary conduct or what the subject considers to be an obligation. ... This use is closely related to both the use of the prefix conjugation to express volition and to its use for consequential results."
מָנוֹחַ	n, m, s, abs מָנוֹחַ √נוח "resting place, state, or condition of rest, security"
אֲשֶׁר	rel pron אֲשֶׁר √אשר "which"
יִיטַב־לָךְ	v, G, impf, juss, 3, m, s √יטב w/ prep לְ w/ 2, f, s, gen sx "it may be good for you"

3:2 וְעַתָּה הֲלֹא בֹעַז מֹדַעְתָּנוּ אֲשֶׁר הָיִית אֶת־נַעֲרוֹתָיו הִנֵּה־הוּא זֹרֶה אֶת־גֹּרֶן הַשְּׂעֹרִים הַלָּיְלָה:

3:2 "But now, is not Boaz, with whose young women you were, our kinsman? Look, he will be winnowing the threshing-floor of barley tonight."

וְעַתָּה	temp adv עַתָּה/עֹנה√ w/ ו disj "But now"
הֲלֹא	neg part לֹא w/ interr ה "not? no?"
בֹעַז	PN "Boaz"
מֹדַעְתָּנוּ	v, H, ptc, f, s, *st. pr.* ידע√ w/ 1, c, pl, gen sx "our kindred, kinship" On the form of the pronominal suffix, which is rare but not unknown, see GKC §91f and BL §29k. According to Joüon §94h, it is found only on particles and prepositions, with the singular exception of this word. Also, according to GKC §141c, "The employment of a substantive as predicate of a noun-clause is especially frequent, either when no corresponding adjective exists (so mostly with words expressing the material; cf. §128o) or when the attribute is intended to receive a certain emphasis." Joüon §89b: "A very small number [of masculine nouns] have a feminine ending.... Here the feminine ending has an intensive nuance like, in Arabic, in the forms such as *rāu̯iat* "(great) storyteller," alongside the simple *rāuiⁿ* "storyteller." ... Alongside מוֹדַע *relative* (Ruth 2:1), מוֹדַעַת (3:2) seems to signify *near relative* (probably masculine, since speaking of a man)." In contrast, BL §77d′ understand this word as "acquaintance" (*Bekanntschaft*), and *HALOT* reads it as "(distant) relative." Berg 2 §26i understands this participle as a substantive, and he is probably right, since it does not agree with its referent noun (בֹעַז m, s PN) in gender. It is not unusual for a participle (e.g., the G active participle כֹּהֵן) to lose all the force of a verbal adjective and to become a substantive.
אֲשֶׁר	rel pron אֲשֶׁר/אשר√ "which"
הָיִית	v, G, pf, 2, f, s היה√ "you were"
אֶת־נַעֲרוֹתָיו	n, f, pl, *st. pr.* נַעֲרָה/נער√ w/ 3, m, s, gen sx and prep אֶת "with his young women"
הִנֵּה־הוּא	dem part הִנֵּה "behold!" w/ indep pers pron, 3, m, s, הוּא "he"; "Behold, he..." On הִנֵּה with a pronoun, see Joüon §102k.
זֹרֶה	v, G, act, ptc, m, s זרה√ "winnow"

אֶת־גֹּרֶן   n, m, s, cs גֹּרֶן √גרן w/ sign def dir obj "threshing-floor of"

הַשְּׂעֹרִים   n, f, pl, abs שְׂעֹרָה √שער w/ def art "barley"

הַלָּיְלָה   n, m, s, abs לַיְלָה √ליל w/ def art "tonight"

3:3 וְרָחַצְתְּ ׀ וָסַ֫כְתְּ וְשַׂמְתְּ שִׂמְלֹתֵךְ [שִׂמְלֹתַיִךְ] עָלַיִךְ וְיָרַדְתִּי [וְיָרַדְתְּ] הַגֹּרֶן אֶל־ תּוֹדְעִי לָאִישׁ עַד כַּלֹּתוֹ לֶאֱכֹל וְלִשְׁתּוֹת:

3:3 "So wash yourself, anoint yourself, put on your scarves, and go down to the threshing-floor. Do not make yourself known to the man until he finishes eating and drinking."

וְרָחַצְתְּ   v, G, pf, 2, f, s √רחץ w/ ו cons "so wash yourself"
On the use of a perfect consecutive to express a command or wish, see GKC §112aa, Berg 2 §9i, and Driver, p. 142.

וָסַ֫כְתְּ   v, G, pf, 2, f, s √סוך w/ ו cons "and anoint yourself"
GKC §104g: "Immediately before the tone-syllable, [the ו] frequently takes *Qameṣ*, like בְּ, כְּ, לְ (see § 102 *f*), but in most cases only at the end of a sentence or clause." On the use of a perfect consecutive to express a command or wish, see GKC §112aa, Berg 2 §9i, and Driver, p. 142.

וְשַׂמְתְּ   v, G, pf, 2, f, s √שים w/ ו cons "and place"
According to BL §56u″, one variant reads וְשַׂמְתִּי, which according to §42k–l is an acceptable variant of the G perfect second feminine singular. According to Joüon §16e, וְשַׂמְתִּי is the archaic form. On the use of a perfect consecutive to express a command or wish, see GKC §112aa, Berg 2 §9i, and Driver, p. 142.

שִׂמְלֹתֵךְ   K, n, f, pl, *st. pr.* שִׂמְלָה √שמל w/ 2, f, s, gen sx "your scarves"

שִׂמְלֹתַיִךְ   Q, n, f, pl, *st. pr.* שִׂמְלָה √שמל w/ 2, f, s, gen sx "your scarves"

עָלַיִךְ   prep עַל √עלה w/ 2, f, s, gen sx "upon yourself"

וְיָרַדְתִּי   K, G, pf, 2, f, s √ירד w/ ו cons "and go down"
On the form of the second feminine singular with *î,* see GKC §44h; BL §55c´, §42k–l, Berg 2 §4a, and Joüon §42f. On the use of a perfect consecutive to express a command or wish, see GKC §112aa, Berg 2 §9i, and Driver, p. 142. On the succession of four perfect consecutives here, see GKC §112c.

וְיָרַדְתְּ   Q, G, pf, 2, f, s √ירד w/ ו cons "and you will go down"

הַגֹּרֶן   n, m, s, abs גֹּרֶן √גרן w/ def art "the threshing-floor"

אַל־תִּוָּדְעִי   v, N, impf, juss, 2, f, s √ידע w/ neg part אַל "do not make yourself known" According to *IBHS* §23.4h, the N stem may have a reflexive nuance. Joüon §132c n. 2, "In certain cases, with a reflexive form, the sense has been able to evolve, e.g., Ruth 3:3 אַל־תִּוָּדְעִי לָאִישׁ *do not make yourself known to this man,* from which *do not be recognized by this man.*"

לָאִישׁ   n, m, s, abs אִישׁ √אנשׁ? w/ prep לְ and def art "to the man"

עַד   prep עַד √עדה "until"

כַּלֹּתוֹ   v, D, inf, cs √כלה w/ 3, m, s, gen sx "his completing"

לֶאֱכֹל   v, G, inf, cs √אכל w/ prep לְ "to eat"

וְלִשְׁתּוֹת   v, G, inf, cs √שׁתה w/ prep לְ and ו conj "and to drink"

3:4 וִיהִי בְשָׁכְבוֹ וְיָדַעַתְּ אֶת־הַמָּקוֹם אֲשֶׁר יִשְׁכַּב־שָׁם וּבָאת וְגִלִּית מַרְגְּלֹתָיו וְשָׁכָבְתִּי [וְשָׁכָבְתְּ] וְהוּא יַגִּיד לָךְ אֵת אֲשֶׁר תַּעֲשִׂין:

3:4 "Then, when he lies down, note the place where he is lying, and go, uncover his legs, and lie down. He will tell you what you should do."

וִיהִי   v, G, impf, juss, 3, m, s √היה w/ ו conj [not cons!] "and may it be"
GKC §109k: "Moreover, in not a few cases, the jussive is used, without any collateral sense, for the ordinary imperfect form, and this occurs not alone in forms, which may arise from a misunderstanding of the defective writing ... but also in shortened forms, such as יְהִי." GKC §112z: "The jussive form form וִיהִי occurs (in the sense described in y) instead of וְהָיָה in [1 Sam 10:5, 2 Sam 5:24 (1 Chr 14:15), 1 Kgs 14:5, Ruth 3:4], although in the first three places a jussive is wholly inadmissible in the context, and even in [Ruth 3:4] (where an admonition follows) וְהָיָה would be expected." Driver states that this is one of only four places where we encounter וִיהִי instead of the expected והיה. He continues, "The verb has the force of a legitimate jussive: יהי is simply prefixed to the adverbial clause in the same manner as וַיְהִי and והיה.... Ruth 3[:4] *and let it be,* when he lieth down, *and observe* (or *that thou* observe) the place where he lieth" (p. 148, observation 3). See also Joüon §119z.

בְשָׁכְבוֹ   v, G, inf, cs √שׁכב w/ 3, m, s, gen sx and prep בְּ "in his lying down"
BL §§48d´´: "The suffixed form of the infinitive *qatalu [the original form of the infinitive construct of stative verbs, e.g., לְשְׁכַּב] has either assimilated to that of the stemform *qutulu [the original form of the infinitive construct of dynamic

verbs, e.g., [לִקְטֹל]: (for שָׁכַב) שָׁכְבְּךָ "your lying down" Deut 6:7, 11:19; Prov 6:22; שָׁכְבוּ Ruth 3:4, or it goes back to the stemform *qātlu* (§12c; cf. the feminine form *qātlatu*, §43g): *šăkbahā > (§§25r, 14v) שִׁכְבָה Gen 19:33, 35." See also Joüon §65b and Berg 2 §14m.

וְיָדַעַתְּ
v, G, pf, 2, f, s √ידע w/ ו cons "know, note"
On the use of a perfect consecutive to express a command or wish, see GKC §112aa and Berg 2 §10f, 2 §10q.

אֶת־הַמָּקוֹם
n, m, s, abs מָקוֹם √קום w/ def art and sign def dir obj "the place"

אֲשֶׁר
rel pron אֲשֶׁר √אשר "that"

יִשְׁכַּב־שָׁם
v, G, impf, indic, 3, m, s √שכב w/ loc adv שָׁם "he will lie down there"

וּבָאת
v, G, pf, 2, f, s √בוא w/ ו cons "and go"
On the use of a perfect consecutive to express a command or wish, see GKC §112aa and Berg 2 §10f, 2 §10q.

וְגִלִּית
v, D, pf, 2, f, s √גלה w/ ו cons "and uncover"
On the use of a perfect consecutive to express a command or wish, see GKC §112aa and Berg 2 §10f, 2 §10q.

מַרְגְּלֹתָיו
n, f, *pl. tan., st. pr.* מַרְגְּלוֹת √רגל w/ 3, m, s, gen sx "his feet-place = the place where his feet are"? "his legs"?

וְשָׁכָבְתִּי
K, G, pf, 2, f, s √שכב w/ ו cons "and lie down"
On the form of the second feminine singular with î, see GKC §44h, Berg 2 §4a, BL §42k–l, and Joüon §42f. On the use of a perfect consecutive to express a command or wish, see GKC §112aa and Berg 2 §10f, 2 §10q.

וְשָׁכָבְתְּ
Q, G, pf, 2, f, s √שכב w/ ו cons "and you will lie down"

וְהוּא
indep pers pron, 3, m, s הוּא w/ ו disj "but he"

יַגִּיד
v, H, impf, indic, 3, m, s √נגד "he will tell"

לָךְ
prep לְ w/ 2, f, s, gen sx "to you"

אֵת אֲשֶׁר
rel pron אֲשֶׁר √אשר w/ sign def dir obj "that which"

תַּעֲשִׂין
v, G, impf, indic, 2, f, s √עשה w/ paragogic *nûn* "you should do"
On paragogic *nûn* ("stuck-on *nûn*"), see *IBHS* §31.7.1a, Joüon §44f, BL §40q, and GKC §47o. According to BL §57i, these forms are examples of an older "full aorist form" that has been superseded by the "short aorist form," that is, those forms without the paragogic *nûn*. Berg 2 §5a lists this as a deviating form; see also 2 §30m. According to Joüon §113m, the imperfect may have a nuance of obligation.

3:5 וַתֹּאמֶר אֵלֶיהָ כֹּל אֲשֶׁר־תֹּאמְרִי [אֵלַי] אֶעֱשֶׂה:

3:5 She said to her, "All that you are saying, I will do."

וַתֹּאמֶר	v, G, impf, indic, 3, f, s √אמר w/ ו cons "and she said"
אֵלֶיהָ	prep אֶל w/ 3, f, s, gen sx "to her"
כֹּל	n, m, s, abs כֹּל√ כלל "all"
	Joüon §125i: "One notices a great liberty in the use of אֶת." We would expect an אֶת before כֹּל אֲשֶׁר־ here; cf. 3:16.
אֲשֶׁר־	rel pron אֲשֶׁר √אשר "that"
תֹּאמְרִי	v, G, impf, indic, 2, f, s √אמר "you are saying"
אֵלַי	Q, prep אֶל w/ 1, c, s, gen sx "to me"
	BL §6m states that, according to the Talmud, there are seven cases in which something is not written but still read: פְּרָת 2 Sam 8:3; אִישׁ 2 Sam 16:23; בָּאִים Jer 31:38; לָהּ Jer 50:29; [כֹּל] אֶת Ruth 2:11; אֵלַי Ruth 3:5, 17. Conversely, there are five cases in which words present in the text are not read: נָא 2 Kgs 5:18; וְאֵת Jer 32:11; ידרך Jer 51:3; חֲמֵשׁ Ezek 48:16; אִם Ruth 3:12.
אֶעֱשֶׂה	v, G, impf, indic, 1, c, s √עשה "I will do"

3:6 וַתֵּרֶד הַגֹּרֶן וַתַּעַשׂ כְּכֹל אֲשֶׁר־צִוַּתָּה חֲמוֹתָהּ:

3:6 So she went down to the threshing-floor and did exactly what her mother-in-law commanded her.

וַתֵּרֶד	v, G, impf, indic, 3, f, s √ירד w/ ו cons "and she went down"
הַגֹּרֶן	n, m, s, abs גֹּרֶן √גרן w/ def art "the threshing-floor"
וַתַּעַשׂ	v, G, impf, indic, 3, f, s √עשה w/ ו cons "and she did, acted"
כְּכֹל	n, m, s, abs כֹּל √כלל w/ prep כְּ "according to all"
אֲשֶׁר־	rel pron אֲשֶׁר √אשר "that"
צִוַּתָּה	v, D, pf, 3, f, s √צוה w/ 3, f, s, acc sx "she commanded her"
	On the form of the verb with the accusative suffix, see GKC §59g and Berg 2 §4f, 2 §30l.

חֲמוֹתָהּ	n, f, s, *st. pr.* חָמוֹת √חמה w/ 3, f, s, gen sx "her mother-in-law"

3:7 וַיֹּאכַל בֹּעַז וַיֵּשְׁתְּ וַיִּיטַב לִבּוֹ וַיָּבֹא לִשְׁכַּב בִּקְצֵה הָעֲרֵמָה וַתָּבֹא בַלָּט וַתְּגַל מַרְגְּלֹתָיו וַתִּשְׁכָּב׃

3:7 Boaz ate, drank, and his heart was glad. He came to lie down at the end of the pile of grain. She came in secret and uncovered his legs and lay down.

וַיֹּאכַל	v, G, impf, indic, 3, m, s √אכל w/ ו cons "and he ate"
בֹּעַז	PN "Boaz"
וַיֵּשְׁתְּ	v, G, impf, indic, 3, m, s √שתה w/ ו cons "and he drank"
וַיִּיטַב	v, G, impf, indic, 3, m, s √יטב w/ ו cons "and it was well"
לִבּוֹ	n, m, s, *st. pr.* לֵב √לבב w/ 3, m, s, gen sx "his heart"
וַיָּבֹא	v, G, impf, indic, 3, m, s √בוא w/ ו cons "and he came"
לִשְׁכַּב	v, G, inf, cs √שכב w/ לְ "to lie down"
בִּקְצֵה	n, m, s, cs קָצֶה √קצה w/ prep בְּ "at the end of"
הָעֲרֵמָה	n, f, s, abs עֲרֵמָה √ערם w/ def art "the heap"
וַתָּבֹא	v, G, impf, indic, 3, f, s √בוא w/ ו cons "and she came"
בַלָּט	n, m, s, abs לָט √לוט w/ def art and prep בְּ "in the secrecy, mystery"
וַתְּגַל	v, D, impf, indic, 3, f, s √גלה w/ ו cons "and she uncovered"
מַרְגְּלֹתָיו	n, f, *pl. tan.*, *st. pr.* מַרְגְּלוֹת √רגל w/ 3, m, s, gen sx "his feet-place = the place where his feet are"? "his legs"?
וַתִּשְׁכָּב	v, G, impf, indic, 3, f, s √שכב w/ ו cons "and she lay down"

3:8 וַיְהִי בַּחֲצִי הַלַּיְלָה וַיֶּחֱרַד הָאִישׁ וַיִּלָּפֵת וְהִנֵּה אִשָּׁה שֹׁכֶבֶת מַרְגְּלֹתָיו׃

3:8 At midnight, the man was startled and twisted himself about, and behold, a woman lying at his feet!

וַיְהִי	v, G, impf, indic, 3, m, s √היה w/ ו cons "and it happened"

בַּחֲצִי   n, m, s, cs חֲצִי√הצה w/ prep בְּ "in the middle of"

הַלַּיְלָה   n, m, s, abs לַיְלָה√ליל w/ def art "the night"

וַיֶּחֱרַד   v, G, impf, indic, 3, m, s חרד√ w/ וּ cons "and he started [= he was startled]"

הָאִישׁ   n, m, s, abs אִישׁ√אנשׁ? w/ def art "the man"

וַיִּלָּפֵת   v, N, impf, indic, 3, m, s לפת√ w/ וּ cons "and he twisted himself about"
On this sense of the N stem, see Wms §135.

וְהִנֵּה   dem part הִנֵּה w/ וּ conj "and behold!"

אִשָּׁה   n, f, s, abs אִשָּׁה√אנשׁ "a woman"

שֹׁכֶבֶת   v, G, act, ptc, f, s שׁכב√ "lying"

מַרְגְּלֹתָיו   n, f, *pl. tan., st. pr.* מַרְגְּלוֹת√רגל w/ 3, m, s, gen sx "his feet-place = the place where his feet are"? "his legs"?
This is an adverbial accusative of place: "at his feet" (*IBHS* §10.2.2). So also Joüon §126h.

3:9 וַיֹּאמֶר מִי־אָתְּ וַתֹּאמֶר אָנֹכִי רוּת אֲמָתֶךָ וּפָרַשְׂתָּ כְנָפֶךָ עַל־אֲמָתְךָ כִּי גֹאֵל אָתָּה:

3:9 He said, "Who are you?" She said, "I am Ruth, your maidservant. You should spread the edge of your garment over your maidservant, since you are a kinsman-redeemer."

וַיֹּאמֶר   v, G, impf, indic, 3, m, s אמר√ w/ וּ cons "and he said"

מִי־אָתְּ   interr pron מִי w/ indep pers pron, 2, f, s (pausal form) אַתְּ√אנת "who are you?"
IBHS §18.2b: "The interrogative use of מִי as a predicate in verbless clauses can serve to elicit an identification ('I am Moses') or a classification ('I am an Israelite')." *BHL* (and the printed editions) restores a simple *shewa* under the תּ, which is missing in L (and *BHS*); see appendix A in *BHL*.

וַתֹּאמֶר   v, G, impf, indic, 3, f, s אמר√ w/ וּ cons "and she said"

אָנֹכִי   indep pers pron, 1, c, s, אָנֹכִי "I"

רוּת   PN "Ruth"

אֲמָתֶךָ   n, f, s, *st. pr.* אָמָה√אמה w/ 2, m, s, gen sx "your maid"

וּפָרַשְׂתָּ   v, G, pf, 2, m, s פרשׂ√ w/ וּ cons "and you should spread out"
According to Joüon §119w, the perfect consecutive, "like the imperfect §113l–n, may have the modal nuances of 'may, ought, want': . . . Ruth 3:9 '*and*

you ought to spread out וּפָרַשְׂתָּ֫' (Ruth declares to Boaz his obligation as *go'el*; cf. v. 12)." The perfect with *wāw* consecutive can also be understood as having imperative force (Driver, p. 142; GKC §112aa; Berg 2 §9i).

כְּנָפֶ֫ךָ	n, m, s, *st. pr.* כָּנָף √כנף w/ 2, m, s, gen sx "your wing, extremity"
עַל־אֲמָתֶ֫ךָ	n, f, s, *st. pr.* אָמָה √אמה w/ 2, m, s, gen sx and prep עַל √עלה "over your maid" Joüon §15k: "of two similar accents, the first is always the stronger. This law appears indeed in Ruth 3:9 where the first *zaqef* has produced the pausal vocalization [under the ת] אֲמָתֶ֫ךָ, but not the second *zaqef* (אֲמָתֶ֫ךָ)."
כִּי	conj כִּי "that, for, when"
גֹאֵל	v, G, act, ptc, m, s, abs √גאל "redeemer"
אָתָּה	indep pers pron, 2, m, s אַתָּה √אנת "you"

3:10 וַיֹּ֗אמֶר בְּרוּכָ֨ה אַ֤תְּ לַֽיהוָה֙ בִּתִּ֔י הֵיטַ֛בְתְּ חַסְדֵּ֥ךְ הָאַחֲר֖וֹן מִן־הָרִאשׁ֑וֹן לְבִלְתִּי־לֶ֣כֶת אַחֲרֵ֣י הַבַּֽחוּרִ֔ים אִם־דַּ֖ל וְאִם־עָשִֽׁיר׃

3:10   He said, "Blessed be you to YHWH, my daughter! You have made this latter act of covenant-loyalty greater than the former by not going after the choice men, whether rich or poor."

וַיֹּ֫אמֶר	v, G, impf, indic, 3, m, s √אמר w/ ו cons "and he said"
בְּרוּכָה	v, G, pass, ptc, f, s, abs √ברך "blessed"
אַתְּ לַֽיהוָה	indep pers pron, 2, f, s אַתְּ √אנת w/ DN "YHWH" w/ prep לְ "are you to YHWH" *IBHS* §11.2.10d: "The quasi-allative [*allative* means direction or motion to or toward] relations involve the *goal* of an action and are largely of the type sometimes called *datival*. The so-called indirect object of verbs of giving and some verbs of speaking and listening takes *l*. They translate בָּרוּךְ הוּא לַיהוה as "May he be pronounced blessed *to* YHWH." In n. 72 they specify "Not 'by'" and reference Pardee, *UF* 8:221–23. This is in contrast to Joüon §132f: "Blessed be he *by* YHWH." *IBHS* is correct.
בִּתִּי	n, f, s, *st. pr.* בַּת √בנה? w/ 1, c, s, gen sx "my daughter"
הֵיטַ֫בְתְּ	v, H, pf, 2, f, s √יטב "make a thing good, right, beautiful"
חַסְדֵּךְ	n, m, s, *st. pr.* חֶ֫סֶד √חסד w/ 2, f, s, gen sx "your covenant-loyalty"

הָאַחֲרוֹן	adj, m, s, abs אַחֲרוֹן √אחר w/ def art "the latter"
מִן־הָרִאשׁוֹן	adj, m, s, abs רִאשׁוֹן √ראשׁ w/ def art and prep מִן "than the former"
לְבִלְתִּי־	neg part בִּלְתִּי (from בֵּלֶת [בלה?]; cf Ugaritic *blt*) w/ לְ used to negate infinitives "not to…"
לֶכֶת	v, G, inf, cs √הלך "going"
אַחֲרֵי	prep "behind, after" (properly n, m, pl, cs אַחַר √אחר "hinder parts of")
הַבַּחוּרִים	n, m, pl, abs בָּחוּר √בחר w/ def art "the chosen ones, i.e., the young men"
אִם־דַּל	adj, m, s, abs דַּל √דלל w/ hypoth part אִם "whether poor"
וְאִם־עָשִׁיר	adj, m, s, abs עָשִׁיר √עשר w/ hypoth part אִם and ו conj "or rich"

3:11 וְעַתָּה בִּתִּי אַל־תִּירְאִי כֹּל אֲשֶׁר־תֹּאמְרִי אֶעֱשֶׂה־לָּךְ כִּי יוֹדֵעַ כָּל־שַׁעַר עַמִּי כִּי אֵשֶׁת חַיִל אָתְּ:

3:11 "But now, my daughter, do not fear. All that you say, I will do for you, since the entire gate of my people knows that you are a woman of excellent character."

וְעַתָּה	temp adv עַתָּה √ענה w/ ו disj "but now"
בִּתִּי	n, f, s, *st. pr.* בַּת √בנה? w/ 1, c, s, gen sx "my daughter"
אַל־תִּירְאִי	v, G, impf, juss, 2, f, s √ירא w/ neg part אַל "do not fear"
כֹּל	n, m, s, abs כֹּל √כלל "all" Joüon §125i: "One notices a great liberty in the use of אֵת." We would expect an אֵת before כֹּל אֲשֶׁר־ here; cf. 3:16.
אֲשֶׁר־	rel pron אֲשֶׁר √אשׁר "that"
תֹּאמְרִי	v, G, impf, indic, 2, f, s √אמר "you may say"
אֶעֱשֶׂה־לָּךְ	v, G, impf, indic, 1, c, s √עשה w/ prep לְ w/ 2, f, s, gen sx "I will do for you"
כִּי	conj כִּי "for, because, that"
יוֹדֵעַ	v, G, act, ptc, m, s, abs √ידע "knowing"
כָּל־שַׁעַר	n, m, s, cs שַׁעַר √שׁער w/ n, m, s, cs, כֹּל √כלל "all of the gate of"
עַמִּי	n, m, s, *st. pr.* עַם √עמם w/ 1, c, s, gen sx "my people"

כִּי	conj כִּי "for, because, that"
אֵשֶׁת	n, f, s, cs √אנש אִשָּׁה "a woman"
חַיִל	n, m, s, abs √חול חַיִל "strength, efficiency, wealth, army" The construct chain can be used instead of an adjectival phrase, so that an abstract noun replaces an adjective; so explains Brock §76d, who translates our phrase "a capable woman." This phrase could also be translated as "a powerful woman" or, if the context allowed it (which it does not here), "a wealthy woman." Perhaps the strength of Ruth's character makes her "a powerful woman."
אַתְּ	indep pers pron, 2, f, s √אנת אַתְּ "you"

3:12 וְעַתָּה כִּי אָמְנָם כִּי אִם גֹּאֵל אָנֹכִי וְגַם יֵשׁ גֹּאֵל קָרוֹב מִמֶּנִּי׃

3:12 "Now, it is indeed true that I am a kinsman-redeemer, but there is also a kinsman-redeemer nearer than I."

וְעַתָּה	temp adv √ענה עַתָּה w/ ו disj "but now"
כִּי	dem part כִּי "indeed" On both uses of כִּי in this verse, see *GAHG* 3:177 n. 605.
אָמְנָם	adv √אמן אָמְנָם "verily, truly"
כִּי	conj כִּי "for, because, that"
אִם	K, hypoth part אִם "if" According to the Masorah, the אִם is written but not read (so Joüon §16e), and BL §6m states that, according to the Talmud, there are seven cases in which something is not written but still read: פְּרָת 2 Sam 8:3; אִישׁ 2 Sam 16:23; בָּאִים Jer 31:38; לָהּ Jer 50:29; [כֹּל] אֶת Ruth 2:11; אֵלַי Ruth 3:5, 17. Conversely, there are five cases in which words present in the text are not read: נָא 2 Kgs 5:18; וְאֶת Jer 32:11; ידרך Jer 51:3; חָמֵשׁ Ezek 48:16; אִם Ruth 3:12. According to GKC §163d, כִּי אִם may introduce an emphatic assurance, "indeed."
גֹּאֵל	v, G, act, ptc, m, s, abs √גאל "a redeemer"
אָנֹכִי	indep pers pron, 1, c, s אָנֹכִי "I"
וְגַם	adv √גמם גַּם w/ ו disj "but also"
יֵשׁ	part of existence יֵשׁ "there is"

IBHS §4.5b: "In a *verbal clause* the predicate is a verb," which may be a finite verb, an infinitive absolute, an infinitive construct, or a quasi-verbal indicator, which includes particles denoting existence. So also Wms §568.

גֹּאֵל   v, G, act, ptc, m, s, abs √גאל "a redeemer"

קָרוֹב   adj, m, s, abs קרב√ קָרוֹב "nearer"

מִמֶּנִּי   prep מִן w/ 1, c, s, gen sx "than me"

3:13 לִינִי ׀ הַלַּיְלָה וְהָיָה בַבֹּקֶר אִם־יִגְאָלֵךְ טוֹב יִגְאָל וְאִם־לֹא יַחְפֹּץ לְגָאֳלֵךְ וּגְאַלְתִּיךְ אָנֹכִי חַי־יְהוָה שִׁכְבִי עַד־הַבֹּקֶר׃

3:13 "Spend the night, and in the morning, if he will redeem you, good! But if he is not pleased to redeem you, then I myself, by the life of YHWH, will redeem you! Lie down until the morning."

לִינִי   v, G, impf, impv, 2, f, s √לון "spend the night!"

הַלַּיְלָה   n, m, s, abs ליל√ לַיְלָה w/ def art "tonight"

וְהָיָה   v, G, pf, 3, m, s √היה w/ ו cons "and it will be"

בַבֹּקֶר   n, m, s, abs בקר√ בֹּקֶר w/ def art and prep בְּ "in the morning"

אִם־יִגְאָלֵךְ   v, G, impf, indic, 3, m, s √גאל w/ 2, m, s, acc sx and hypoth part אִם "if he will redeem you"
According to Joüon §113n, the imperfect can have a nuance of *want to:* "Ruth 3:13 '*if he wants to buy you back* (in the second member explicitly וְאִם־לֹא יַחְפֹּץ *and if he does not want*).'" On conditional clauses in general, see Joüon §167.

טוֹב   adj, m, s, abs טוב√ טוֹב "good!"

יִגְאָל   v, G, impf, juss, 3, m, s גאל√ "let him redeem"

וְאִם־לֹא   hypoth part אִם w/ neg part and ו disj "but if not"

יַחְפֹּץ   v, G, impf, indic, 3, m, s √חפץ "he will be pleased"

לְגָאֳלֵךְ   v, G, inf, cs √גאל w/ 2, f, s, acc sx and prep לְ "to redeem you"

וּגְאַלְתִּיךְ   v, G, pf, 1, c, s √גאל w/ 2, f, s, acc sx and ו cons "then I will redeem you"

אָנֹכִי   indep pers pron, 1, c, s אָנֹכִי "I"

חַי־יְהוָה	n, m, s, cs √חיה חַי w/ DN "YHWH"; "by the life of YHWH"
שִׁכְבִי	v, G, impf, impv, 2, f, s √שׁכב "lie down!"
עַד־הַבֹּקֶר	n, m, s, abs בֹּקֶר √בקר w/ def art and prep עַד √עדה "until the morning"

3:14 וַתִּשְׁכַּב מַרְגְּלָתוֹ [מַרְגְּלוֹתָיו] עַד־הַבֹּקֶר וַתָּקָם בְּטֶרוֹם [בְּטֶרֶם] יַכִּיר אִישׁ אֶת־רֵעֵהוּ וַיֹּאמֶר אַל־יִוָּדַע כִּי־בָאָה הָאִשָּׁה הַגֹּרֶן:

3:14   So she lay down at his feet until the morning, then she got up before a man could recognize his neighbor. He said, "May it not be known that the woman came to the threshing-floor."

וַתִּשְׁכַּב	v, G, impf, indic, 3, f, s √שׁכב w/ ו cons "so she lay down"
מַרְגְּלָתוֹ	K, n, f, s, *st. pr.* מַרְגְּלָה √רגל w/ 3, m, s, gen sx "at his foot"
מַרְגְּלוֹתָיו	Q, n, f, *pl. tan., st. pr.* מַרְגְּלוֹת √רגל w/ 3, m, s, gen sx "his feet-place = the place where his feet are"? "his legs"?
עַד־הַבֹּקֶר	n, m, s, abs בֹּקֶר √בקר w/ def art and prep עַד √עדה "until the morning"
וַתָּקָם	v, G, impf, indic, 3, f, s √קום w/ ו cons "and she got up"
בְּטֶרוֹם	K, temp adv טֶרוֹם w/ prep בְּ "before"
בְּטֶרֶם	Q, temp adv טֶרֶם w/ prep בְּ "before"
יַכִּיר	v, H, impf, indic, 3, m, s √נכר "he could recognize" According to GKC §107b, the imperfect is often used to express actions that "*continued* throughout a long or shorter period [107c] after the particle … בְּטֶרֶם before." Berg 2 §7i: "The imperfect frequently expresses, besides its tense significance, still other modifications of the meaning" that require modal verbs such as *can, may, want, intend,* and *must* to render the thought into English. He adds in the next paragraph (k): "the use of the imperfect treated in [the last paragraph] is not limited to the present but can refer also to the future and especially, in connection with phrases for the past, to the past" (such as here in our verse, which Berg cites).
אִישׁ	n, m, s, abs אִישׁ √אנשׁ? "each"
אֶת־רֵעֵהוּ	n, m, s, *st. pr.* רֵעַ √רעה w/ 3, m, s, gen sx and sign def dir obj "his neighbor"
וַיֹּאמֶר	v, G, impf, indic, 3, m, s √אמר w/ ו cons "and he said"

אַל־יִוָּדַ֕ע	v, N, impf, juss, 3, m, s √ידע w/ neg part אַל "may it not be known"
כִּי־בָ֥אָה	v, G, pf, 3, f, s √בוא w/ conj כִּי "that she came"
הָאִשָּׁ֖ה	n, f, s, abs אִשָּׁה √אנש w/ def art "the woman"
הַגֹּֽרֶן	n, m, s, abs גֹּרֶן √גרן w/ def art "the threshing-floor"

3:15 וַיֹּ֗אמֶר הָ֠בִי הַמִּטְפַּ֧חַת אֲשֶׁר־עָלַ֛יִךְ וְאֶחֳזִי־בָ֖הּ וַתֹּ֣אחֶז בָּ֑הּ וַיָּ֤מָד שֵׁשׁ־שְׂעֹרִים֙ וַיָּ֣שֶׁת עָלֶ֔יהָ וַיָּבֹ֖א הָעִֽיר:

3:15   He said, "Take the cloak that you have on and hold it out." She held it out and he measured six measures of barley and put them on it. Then he entered the city.

וַיֹּ֗אמֶר	v, G, impf, indic, 3, m, s √אמר w/ ו cons "and he said"
הָ֠בִי	v, G, impf, impv, 2, f, s √יהב "give!" On the form of this imperative, see GKC §69o and BL §83f (who calls this an interjection). Brock §6a states that the root יהב, inflected as an imperative, often introduces a volitive clause, and he translates our clause: "here with your shawl and hold it." Berg 2 §29d indicates that there is a Q הָבִיא (H infinitive construct of בוא "bring") but that the K (הָבִי) is to be read. Neither *BHL* nor *BHS* nor L have this Kethib-Qere variant.
הַמִּטְפַּ֧חַת	n, f, s, abs מִטְפַּחַת √טפח w/ def art "the cloak"
אֲשֶׁר־עָלַ֛יִךְ	rel pron אֲשֶׁר √אשר and prep עַל √עלה w/ 2, f, s, gen sx "that is on you"
וְאֶחֳזִי־בָ֖הּ	v, G, impf, impv, 2, f, s √אחז w/ prep בְּ w/ 3, f, s, gen sx and ו conj "and hold it" This form of the imperative is a slight deviation from the ordinary inflexion (GKC §64c; BL §53v). On the *sĕgōl* under the א, see BL §49g; on the *ḥāṭēp paṭaḥ* under the ח, see BL §50c. See also Jouön §69b and Berg 1 §28k, 2 §21k.
וַתֹּ֣אחֶז	v, G, impf, indic, 3, f, s √אחז w/ ו cons "so she held"
בָּ֑הּ	prep בְּ w/ 3, f, s, gen sx "it"
וַיָּ֤מָד	v, G, impf, indic, 3, m, s √מדד w/ ו cons "and he measured"
שֵׁשׁ־שְׂעֹרִים֙	n, m, s, abs שֵׁשׁ √שדש "six" and n, f, pl, abs שְׂעֹרָה √שער "barley" = "six units of barley" According to *IBHS* §15.2.2b, שֵׁשׁ is absolute, and "the unit words for commodities may be omitted." They translate, "six (*ephahs of*) barley." On this last point, so also Brock §85e, GKC §134n, Jouön §142n, and Wms §590.

וַיָּ֫שֶׁת	v, G, impf, indic, 3, m, s √שׁית w/ ו cons "and he put"
עָלֶ֫יהָ	prep עַל√ עלה w/ 3, f, s, gen sx "upon her"
וַיָּבֹא	v, G, impf, indic, 3, m, s √בוא w/ ו cons "and he entered"
הָעִֽיר	n, f, s, abs עִיר w/ def art "the city"

3:16 וַתָּבוֹא֙ אֶל־חֲמוֹתָ֔הּ וַתֹּ֖אמֶר מִי־אַ֣תְּ בִּתִּ֑י וַתַּ֨גֶּד־לָ֔הּ אֵ֛ת כָּל־אֲשֶׁ֥ר עָֽשָׂה־לָ֖הּ הָאִֽישׁ׃

3:16   She came to her mother-in-law, and she said, "What of you, my daughter?" She related to her all that the man did for her.

וַתָּבוֹא֙	v, G, impf, indic, 3, f, s √בוא w/ ו cons "and she came"
אֶל־חֲמוֹתָ֔הּ	n, f, s, *st. pr.* חָמוֹת √חמה w/ 3, f, s, gen sx and prep אֶל "to her mother-in-law"
וַתֹּ֖אמֶר	v, G, impf, indic, 3, f, s √אמר w/ ו cons "and she said"
מִי־אַ֣תְּ	interr pron מִי w/ indep pers pron, 2, f, s, אַתְּ √אנת "who are you?" *IBHS* §18.2d: "Most occurrences of מִי refer to persons in a straightforward way, but some are not so clear. When a thing is closely associated with the person or is pregnant with the idea of a person, or where persons are understood and implied, מִי may be used. For example, 'What is your name?' can be expressed by מִי שְׁמֶ֫ךָ, because the name is conceived of as a surrogate for the person. Because the inquiry, however, is about some thing … or condition …, English idiom requires other interrogatives" (e.g., what, how, where). They translate this clause, "*Who* are you (i.e., *How* did it go)?"
בִּתִּ֑י	n, f, s, *st. pr.* בַּת √בנה? w/ 1, c, s, gen sx "my daughter"
וַתַּ֨גֶּד־לָ֔הּ	v, G, impf, indic, 3, f, s √נגד w/ prep לְ w/ 3, f, s, gen sx and ו cons "and she reported to her"
אֵ֛ת כָּל־	n, m, s, cs כֹּל √כלל w/ sign def dir obj "all that" Joüon §125i: "One notices a great liberty in the use of אֵת." We have an אֵת before כָּל־אֲשֶׁר here, but compare 3:5, 11.
אֲשֶׁ֥ר	rel pron אֲשֶׁר √אשׁר "that"
עָֽשָׂה־לָ֖הּ	v, G, pf, 3, m, s √עשׂה w/ prep לְ w/ 3, f, s, gen sx "he did for her"
הָאִֽישׁ	n, m, s, abs אִישׁ √אנשׁ? w/ def art "the man"

3:17 וַתֹּאמֶר שֵׁשׁ־הַשְּׂעֹרִים הָאֵלֶּה נָתַן לִי כִּי אָמַר [אֵלַי] אַל־תָּבוֹאִי רֵיקָם אֶל־חֲמוֹתֵךְ:

3:17 She said, "He gave me these six measures of barley, for he said to me, 'Do not come empty-handed to your mother-in-law.'"

וַתֹּאמֶר	v, G, impf, indic, 3, f, s √אמר w/ ו cons "and she said"
שֵׁשׁ־הַשְּׂעֹרִים	n, m, s, abs שֵׁשׁ √שׁדשׁ "six" and n, f, pl, abs שְׂעֹרָה √שׁער "barley" = "six units of barley" According to *IBHS* §15.2.2b, שֵׁשׁ is absolute, and "the unit words for commodities may be omitted." They translate the same clause in 3:15 as "*six (ephahs of)* barley." On this last point, so also GKC §134n, Joüon §142n, and Wms §590.
הָאֵלֶּה	dem adj, prox, m, pl אֵלֶּה w/ def art "these"
נָתַן	v, G, pf, 3, m, s √נתן "he gave"
לִי	prep לְ w/ 1, c, s, gen sx "to me"
כִּי	conj כִּי "for, because, that"
אָמַר	v, G, pf, 3, m, s √אמר "he said"
אֵלַי	Q, prep אֶל w/ 1, c, s, gen sx "to me" According to the Talmud, there are seven cases in which something is not written but still read: פְּרָת 2 Sam 8:3; אִישׁ 2 Sam 16:23; בָּאִים Jer 31:38; לָהּ Jer 50:29; [כֹּל] אֵת Ruth 2:11; אֵלַי Ruth 3:5, 17. Conversely, there are five cases in which words present in the text are not read: נָא 2 Kgs 5:18; וְאֵת Jer 32:11; ידרך Jer 51:3; חֲמֵשׁ Ezek 48:16; אִם Ruth 3:12 (BL §6m; so also Joüon §16e).
אַל־תָּבוֹאִי	v, G, impf, juss, 2, f, s √בוא w/ neg part "don't come" Joüon §114j: "The jussive is employed in a rather broad fashion, e.g., … Ruth 3:17 *it is not necessary that you return empty-handed* (here the action depends on him who speaks)." *IBHS* §34.3b adds, "The sense of a jussive in simple discourse usually follows from the status relations of the speaker and addressee. When a superior uses the jussive with reference to an inferior the volitional force may be command…, exhortation…, counsel…, or invitation or permission."
רֵיקָם	adv רֵיקָם √ריק "empty-handed"
אֶל־חֲמוֹתֵךְ	n, f, s, *st. pr.* חָמוֹת √חמה w/ 2, f, s, gen sx and prep אֶל "to your mother-in-law"

3:18 וַתֹּאמֶר שְׁבִי בִתִּי עַד אֲשֶׁר תֵּדְעִין אֵיךְ יִפֹּל דָּבָר כִּי לֹא יִשְׁקֹט הָאִישׁ כִּי־אִם־כִּלָּה הַדָּבָר הַיּוֹם:

3:18   Then she said, "Sit, my daughter, until you know how it turns out, for the man will not rest unless he has finished the matter today."

וַתֹּאמֶר	v, G, impf, indic, 3, f, s √אמר w/ ו cons "and she said"
שְׁבִי	v, G, impf, impv, 2, f, s √ישב "sit!"
בִתִּי	n, f, s, *st. pr.* בַּת √בנה? w/ 1, c, s, gen sx "my daughter"
עַד	prep עַד √עדה "until"
אֲשֶׁר	rel pron אֲשֶׁר √אשר "that"
תֵּדְעִין	v, G, impf, indic, 2, f, s √ידע w/ paragogic *nûn* "you know" On paragogic *nûn* ("stuck-on *nûn*"), see *IBHS* §31.7.1a, Joüon §44f, BL §40q, and GKC §47o. Berg 2 §5a lists this as a deviating form.
אֵיךְ	interr adv אֵיךְ "how?"
יִפֹּל	v, G, impf, indic, 3, m, s √נפל "it will fall"
דָּבָר	n, m, s, abs דָּבָר √דבר "the thing" The expected definite article is inexplicably missing (Joüon §137p n. 2).
כִּי	conj כִּי "for, because, that"
לֹא יִשְׁקֹט	v, G, impf, indic, 3, m, s √שקט w/ neg part לֹא "he will not be quiet, undisturbed"
הָאִישׁ	n, m, s, abs אִישׁ √אנש? w/ def art "the man"
כִּי־אִם־	hypoth part אִם "if" + conj כִּי "for" = "unless" GKC §163c: "*Exceptive* clauses, depending on another sentence, are introduced by אֶפֶס כִּי *except that,* and (again after negative sentences, see a above) כִּי אִם *unless;* especially כִּי אִם with the perfect (equivalent to *unless previously*) after imperfects which contain a declaration" (listing Ruth 3:18 as an example). They explain in n. 1: "Very probably this use of כִּי אִם arises from the original meaning *for if, surely if* (כִּי in an affirmative sense).... When the exception follows, an ellipse must be assumed, e.g. [Ruth 3:18] *surely* (or *for*) *when he has finished it* (then the man will rest). It is far less natural to assume such an ellipse with כִּי אִם *but* (before entire clauses as before single nouns); see a above." So also Joüon §173b.

כִּלָּה   v, D, pf, 3, m, s √כלה "he has finished"

הַדָּבָר   n, m, s, abs דָּבָר √דבר w/ def art "the thing"

הַיּוֹם   n, m, s, abs יוֹם w/ def art "today"

RUTH 4:1–22

4:1 וּבֹעַז עָלָה הַשַּׁעַר֩ וַיֵּ֨שֶׁב שָׁ֜ם וְהִנֵּ֣ה הַגֹּאֵ֣ל עֹבֵ֗ר אֲשֶׁ֤ר דִּבֶּר־בֹּ֙עַז֙ וַיֹּ֣אמֶר ס֣וּרָה שְׁבָה־פֹּ֖ה פְּלֹנִ֣י אַלְמֹנִ֑י וַיָּ֖סַר וַיֵּשֵׁב׃

4:1 Now Boaz went up to the gate and sat there just as the kinsman-redeemer about whom he had spoken was passing by. Boaz said, "Come over and sit here, so-and-so." He turned aside and sat down.

וּבֹעַז	PN w/ ו disj "now Boaz" On disjunctive *wāw* introducing a new subject, see Vance §11.3; *IBHS* §39.2.3c.
עָלָה	v, G, pf, 3, m, s √עלה "he went up"
הַשַּׁעַר	n, m, s, abs √שַׁעַר שער w/ def art "the gate"
וַיֵּשֶׁב	v, G, impf, indic, 3, m, s √ישב w/ ו cons "and he sat down"
שָׁם	loc adv שָׁם "there"
וְהִנֵּה	dem part הִנֵּה w/ ו conj "and behold! [≈ just as]" A participial clause introduced by הִנֵּה may form a circumstantial clause denoting action contemporaneous with the main clause (*IBHS* §37.6d; GKC §116o).
הַגֹּאֵל	v, G, act, ptc, m, s, abs √גאל w/ def art "the redeemer"
עֹבֵר	v, G, act, ptc, m, s, abs √עבר "was passing by" On a participle expressing past time, see Berg 2 §13e.
אֲשֶׁר	rel pron אֲשֶׁר √אשר "of whom " Joüon §158i; "With the *verbs of speech,* the preposition signifying *the object of the speech* (בְּ, לְ, עַל) is often omitted" before the retrospective pronoun.

דִּבֶּר־	v, D, pf, 3, m, s √דבר "he spoke"
בֹּעַז	PN "Boaz"
וַיֹּאמֶר	v, G, impf, indic, 3, m, s √אמר w/ ו cons "and he said"
סוּרָה	v, G, impf, impv, 2, m, s w/ volitive ה ֶ √סור "turn aside"
שְׁבָה־פֹּה	v, G, impf, impv, 2, m, s w/ volitive ה ֶ √ישׁב w/ loc adv פֹּה "sit here"

Joüon §177e: "With the imperative, one very often has the asyndetic construction when the second verb follows immediately; in other words, one much more often has the type לֵךְ אֱמֹר *go, say* (= go say) than לֵךְ וְאֱמֹר."

פְּלֹנִי אַלְמֹנִי	Always together, the words of this phrase occur only here and in 1 Sam 21:3; 2 Kgs 6:8 (places in both). It means "such-and-such" or "so-and-so." The etymology is unknown, but see BL §34a, who writes: "perhaps a reformation … from אַל־מֹנֶה*, *not counted, not named*." Brock §24c: "Should the name of a person not be stated, then it is replaced by פְּלֹנִי (whose original meaning is no longer recognized), often in combination with אַלְמֹנִי, as in שְׁבָה־פֹּה פְּלֹנִי אַלְמֹנִי 'take a seat here, [name unknown].' Ruth 4:1." Joüon §147f explains: "*Such*, in place of a noun which is not expressed, is rendered by פְּלֹנִי אַלְמֹנִי Ruth 4:1." *DCH* (s.v. אַלְמֹנִי) remark, "only in פְּלֹנִי אַלְמֹנִי *such and such, so and so*, unnamed place or person." Because the only other occurences of this phrase are references to places, *DCH* suggests as an alternative for our verse "sit here [in] such and such [a place]." *HALOT* (s.v. אַלְמֹנִי) states, "trad[itionally from] I אלם *dumb* = *unknown* … formally connected with פְּלֹנִי which always precedes: *a certain* place, man"; [s.v. פְּלֹנִי] "*someone or other, someone not known*."
וַיָּסַר	v, G, impf, indic, 3, m, s √סור w/ ו cons "and he turned aside"

The *pataḥ* under the gutteral is due to the influence of the gutteral-like ר (GKC §72t; Berg 1 §28c). Although this form could be parsed as an H ("and he removed"), the context requires the sense of the G; so also GKC §72t.

וַיֵּשֵׁב	v, G, impf, indic, 3, m, s √ישׁב w/ ו cons "and he sat down"

This is a pausal form (see GKC §69p; Berg 2 §26b).

4:2 וַיִּקַּח עֲשָׂרָה אֲנָשִׁים מִזִּקְנֵי הָעִיר וַיֹּאמֶר שְׁבוּ־פֹה וַיֵּשֵׁבוּ:

4:2 He took ten men from the elders of the city and said, "Sit here"; and they sat down.

וַיִּקַּח	v, G, impf, indic, 3, m, s √לקח w/ ו cons "and he took"

עֲשָׂרָה   card, f, s, abs עֶ֫שֶׂר√ "ten"

אֲנָשִׁים   n, m, pl, abs אֲנָשִׁים אנשׁ√ (pl by suppletion of אִישׁ אנשׁ√?) "men"

מִזִּקְנֵי   adj, m, pl, cs זָקֵן זקן√ w/ prep מִן "from the elders of"

הָעִיר   n, f, s, abs עִיר√ w/ def art "the city"

וַיֹּאמֶר   v, G, impf, indic, 3, m, s אמר√ w/ ו cons "and he said"

שְׁבוּ־פֹּה   v, G, impf, impv, 2, m, pl ישׁב√ w/ loc adv פֹּה "sit here"

וַיֵּשֵׁבוּ   v, G, impf, indic, 3, m, pl ישׁב√ w/ ו cons "and they sat down"

4:3 וַיֹּ֫אמֶר לַגֹּאֵל חֶלְקַת הַשָּׂדֶה אֲשֶׁר לְאָחִינוּ לֶאֱלִימֶלֶךְ מָכְרָה נָעֳמִי הַשָּׁבָה מִשְּׂדֵה מוֹאָב:

4:3   Then he said to the kinsman-redeemer, "As for the plot of the field that belonged to our relative Elimelech, Naomi, who has just returned from Moab, has decided to sell."

וַיֹּ֫אמֶר   v, G, impf, indic, 3, m, s אמר√ w/ ו cons "and he said"

לַגֹּאֵל   v, G, act, ptc, m, s, abs גאל√ w/ def art and prep לְ "to the redeemer"

חֶלְקַת   n, f, s, cs חֶלְקָה חלק√ "plot, portion of ground"

הַשָּׂדֶה   n, m, s, abs שָׂדֶה שׂדה√ w/ def art "the field"

אֲשֶׁר   rel pron אֲשֶׁר אשׁר√ "which"

לְאָחִינוּ   n, m, s, *st. pr.* אָח אחה√ w/ 1, c, pl, gen sx and prep לְ "to our brother, relative"
GKC §129h: "The periphrastic expression of the genitive by means of אֲשֶׁר לְ is used principally to state the *possessor* ... when a genitive ... is added to a compound, which expresses one united idea" (e.g., Ruth 4:3).

לֶאֱלִימֶלֶךְ   PN w/ prep לְ "to Elimelech"

מָכְרָה   v, G, pf, 3, f, s מכר√ "she has resolved to sell"
IBHS §30.5.1d: "Another present-time use of the suffix conjugation is the *perfective of resolve....* Naomi is going to sell." Similarly, Driver understands the perfect here as being "employed to indicate actions the accomplishment of which lies indeed in the future, but is regarded as dependent upon such an unalterable determination of the will that it may be spoken of as having actually taken place: thus a resolution, promise, or decree, especially a Divine one,

is frequently announced in the perfect tense. A striking instance is afforded by Ruth 4:3, where Boʿaz, speaking of Noʿŏmi's determination to sell her land, says, מָכְרָה נָעֳמִי lit. *has sold* (has resolved to sell: the Engl. idiom would be *is selling*)" (p. 17). This usage is not to be confused with Driver's *prophetic perfect,* which he describes at great length in the next section.

נָעֳמִי   PN "Naomi"

הַשָּׁבָה   v, G, pf, 3, f, s √שוב w/ def art "who returned"
According to GKC §138k, although the Masorah requires that הַשָּׁבָה be parsed as a perfect (because of the tone on the first syllable) and in spite of the fact that the definite article (functioning as a relative pronoun, see GKC §138g) with a perfect is not unheard of, the author probably intended a participle, which requires only the shifting of the accent to the end of the word; so also Joüon §145e. *IBHS* §19.7d: "However the pointing or accentuation in the Masorah is to be explained, such forms should probably be read as participles; the article with the perfective is unlikely in early texts."

מִשְּׂדֵה   n, m, s, cs שָׂדֶה √שדה w/ prep מִן "from the region of"

מוֹאָב   GN "Moab"

4:4 וַאֲנִי אָמַרְתִּי אֶגְלֶה אָזְנְךָ לֵאמֹר קְנֵה נֶגֶד הַיֹּשְׁבִים וְנֶגֶד זִקְנֵי עַמִּי אִם־תִּגְאַל גְּאָל וְאִם־לֹא יִגְאַל הַגִּידָה לִּי וְאֵדַע [וְאֵדְעָה] כִּי אֵין זוּלָתְךָ לִגְאוֹל וְאָנֹכִי אַחֲרֶיךָ וַיֹּאמֶר אָנֹכִי אֶגְאָל:

4:4 "But as for me, I said I would inform you by saying, 'Buy in the presence of the inhabitants and in the presence of the elders of my people.' If you are going to redeem, redeem, but if you are not going to redeem, tell me so that I may know, for there is none except you to redeem, but I am next in line after you." He said, "I, myself, will redeem."

וַאֲנִי   indep pers pron, 1, c, s אֲנִי w/ ו disj "but as for me"

אָמַרְתִּי   v, G, pf, 1, c, s √אמר "I said"

אֶגְלֶה   v, G, impf, indic, 1, c, s √גלה "I will uncover"

אָזְנְךָ   n, f, s, *st. pr.* אֹזֶן √אזן w/ 2, m, s, gen sx "your ear"

לֵאמֹר   v, G, inf, cs √אמר w/ prep לְ "saying"

קְנֵ֣ה   v, G, impf, impv, 2, m, s √קנה "buy"
IBHS §30.5.1d n. 15 implies that this imperative carries the force, "buy here and now."

נֶגֶד   prep נֶגֶד √נגד "in front of, in sight of, opposite to"

הַיֹּשְׁבִ֗ים   v, G, act, ptc, m, pl, abs √ישב w/ def art "the inhabitants"

וְנֶגֶד   prep נֶגֶד √נגד w/ ו conj "and in front of, in sight of, opposite to"

זִקְנֵי   adj, m, pl, cs זָקֵן √זקן "the elders of"

עַמִּ֑י   n, m, s, *st. pr.* עַם √עמם w/ 1, c, s, gen sx "my people"
Joüon §132g: "In the case of apposition, generally the preposition (or אֵת) is repeated when the apposed noun is more precise, more determined than the first noun (cf. §131i); it is not repeated in the contrary case (cf. §131j). In the case of enumeration, when several nouns are governed logically by a preposition, this is often repeated." Thus Joüon would understand this as "the elders of my people seated here," that is, one group of people rather than two, "the inhabitants and the elders of my people." This understanding is precluded by 4:9.

אִם־תִּגְאַל   v, G, impf, indic, 2, m, s √גאל w/ hypoth part אִם "if you are going to redeem"
According to Joüon §113n, the imperfect can have a nuance of "want to," which would here be translated, "If if you want to buy back" (so also Berg 2 §7i).

גְּאָ֔ל   v, G, impf, impv, 2, m, s √גאל "redeem!"
On the pausal lengthening, see GKC §29i n. 1.

וְאִם־לֹא   neg part לֹא w/ hypoth part אִם w/ ו disj "but if not"

יִגְאַל   v, G, impf, indic, 3, m, s √גאל "may he redeem" Read w/ MSS, תִּגְאַל, G impf, indic, 2, m, s √גאל "you will redeem"

הַגִּ֣ידָה   v, H, impf, impv, 2, m, s √נגד w/ volitive הָ "tell"

לִי   prep לְ w/ 1, c, s, gen sx "to me"

וְאֵדַע   K, G, impf, indic, 1, c, s √ידע w/ ו conj "so that I may know"
Berg 2 §10o says that a cohortative sense is intended here, as the Q indicates.

וְאֵדְעָה֙   Q, G, impf, coh, 1, c, s √ידע w/ ו conj "so that I may know"

כִּי   conj כִּי "for, because, that"

אֵין   neg part of existence אַיִן √אין "there is none"
On this absolute use of אַיִן, see GKC §152o.

זוּלָתֵךְ	n, f, s, *st. pr.* זוּלָה √זול functioning as prep w/ 2, m, s, gen sx "except you, only you, save that you" On the presence of a substantive in the construction אֵין plus an infinitive, see Berg 2 §11l.
לִגְאוֹל	v, G, inf, cs √גאל w/ prep לְ "to redeem" According to *IBHS* §36.2.3f, this is a *modal* use of לְ, and they translate: "And none has the right to redeem (it) except you." See also GKC §114l n. 5.
וְאָנֹכִי	indep pers pron, 1, c, s אָנֹכִי w/ ו disj "but I"
אַחֲרֶיךָ	prep "behind, after" (properly n, m, pl, cs אַחַר √אחר "hinder parts of") w/ 2, m, s, gen sx "after you"
וַיֹּאמֶר	v, G, impf, indic, 3, m, s √אמר w/ ו cons "and he said"
אָנֹכִי	indep pers pron, 1, c, s אָנֹכִי "I"
אֶגְאָל	v, G, impf, indic, 1, c, s √גאל "I will redeem" According to Joüon §112f, replying in the imperfect is less "firm and definite" than if the kinsman-redeemer had responded גָּאַלְתִּי, that is, in the perfect: "I hereby redeem." Compare Boaz's speech in 4:9, which is in the perfect.

4:5 וַיֹּאמֶר בֹּעַז בְּיוֹם־קְנוֹתְךָ הַשָּׂדֶה מִיַּד נָעֳמִי וּמֵאֵת רוּת הַמּוֹאֲבִיָּה אֵשֶׁת־הַמֵּת קָנִיתִי [קָנִיתָה] לְהָקִים שֵׁם־הַמֵּת עַל־נַחֲלָתוֹ:

4:5 Then Boaz said, "On the day you buy the field from Naomi, you also buy Ruth, the Moabitess, the wife of the deceased, to raise up the name of the deceased over his estate."

וַיֹּאמֶר	v, G, impf, indic, 3, m, s √אמר w/ ו cons "and he said"
בֹּעַז	PN "Boaz"
בְּיוֹם־	n, m, s, cs יוֹם w/ prep בְּ "in the day of"
קְנוֹתְךָ	v, G, inf, cs √קנה w/ 2, m, s, gen sx "your buying"
הַשָּׂדֶה	n, m, s, abs שָׂדֶה √שדה w/ def art "the field"
מִיַּד	n, f, s, cs יָד w/ prep מִן "from the hand of"
נָעֳמִי	PN "Naomi"
וּמֵאֵת	prep אֵת w/ prep מִן w/ ו conj "and from"

but better is

sign def dir obj w/ וְ conj and enclitic *mêm* "and also"

An enclitic (i.e., never free-standing) *mêm* is a conjunction functioning here as something like "also." *IBHS* §39.2 n. 2 regards וּמֵאֵת as the conjunction *wāw* plus the enclitic *mêm* with the sign of the definite direct object. This changes the understanding of the verse to "And Boaz said, 'On the day that you purchase the field from the hand of Naomi, you also purchase Ruth, the Moabitess, the wife of the dead man, in order to raise up the dead man's name over his estate.'" In support of this understanding, see 4:10 below. Driver emends וּמֵאֵת to גַּם אֶת, as in 4:10 (p. 154).

רוּת	PN "Ruth"
הַמּוֹאֲבִיָּה	gent adj, f, s, abs מוֹאֲבִיָּה (m, s מוֹאָבִי) w/ def art "the Moabitess"
אֵשֶׁת־	n, f, s, cs אִשָּׁה √אנש "the wife of"
הַמֵּת	v, G, act, ptc, m, s, abs √מות w/ def art "the deceased"
קָנִיתִי	K, G, pf, 1, c, s √קנה "I have bought"
קָנִיתָה	Q, G, pf, 2, m, s √קנה "you have bought" Driver understands this perfect as: "thou *wilt have* purchased" (p. 154).
לְהָקִים	v, H, inf, cs √קום w/ prep לְ "the raising up of"
שֵׁם־	n, m, s, cs שֵׁם "the name of"
הַמֵּת	v, G, act, ptc, m, s, abs √מות w/ def art "the deceased"
עַל־נַחֲלָתוֹ	n, f, s, *st. pr.* נַחֲלָה √נחל w/ 3, m, s, gen sx and prep עַל √עלה "over his estate"

4:6 וַיֹּאמֶר הַגֹּאֵל לֹא אוּכַל לִגְאוֹל [לִגְאָל־]לִי פֶּן־אַשְׁחִית אֶת־נַחֲלָתִי גְּאַל־לְךָ אַתָּה אֶת־גְּאֻלָּתִי כִּי לֹא־אוּכַל לִגְאֹל׃

4:6 And the kinsman-redeemer said, "I am not able to redeem for myself, lest I jeopardize my own estate. You redeem my right of redemption for yourself, for I am not able to redeem."

וַיֹּאמֶר	v, G, impf, indic, 3, m, s √אמר w/ וְ cons "and he said"
הַגֹּאֵל	v, G, act, ptc, m, s, abs √גאל w/ def art "the redeemer"
לֹא אוּכַל	v, G, impf, indic, 1, c, s √יכל w/ neg part לֹא "I am not able"

לִגְאוֹל	K, G, inf, cs √גאל "to redeem"
לִגְאָל־	Q, G, inf, cs √גאל "to redeem"
לִי	prep לְ w/ 1, c, s, gen sx "to me"
פֶּן־אַשְׁחִית	v, H, impf, indic, 1, c, s √שחת w/ conj פֶּן "lest I ruin, jeopardize"
אֶת־נַחֲלָתִי	n, f, s, *st. pr.* נַחֲלָה√ נחל w/ 1, c, s, gen sx and sign def dir obj "my estate"
גְּאַל־לְךָ	v, G, impf, impv, 2, m, s √גאל w/ prep לְ w/ 2, m, s, gen sx "redeem!"
אַתָּה	indep pers pron, 2, m, s אַתָּה√ אנת "you"
אֶת־גְּאֻלָּתִי	n, f, s, *st. pr.* גְּאֻלָּה√ גאל w/ 1, c, s, gen sx "my right of redemption"
כִּי	conj כִּי "for, because, that"
לֹא־אוּכַל	v, G, impf, indic, 1, c, s √יכל w/ neg part לֹא "I am not able"
לִגְאֹל	v, G, inf, cs √גאל w/ prep לְ "to redeem"

4:7 וְזֹאת לְפָנִים בְּיִשְׂרָאֵל עַל־הַגְּאוּלָּה וְעַל־הַתְּמוּרָה לְקַיֵּם כָּל־דָּבָר שָׁלַף אִישׁ נַעֲלוֹ וְנָתַן לְרֵעֵהוּ וְזֹאת הַתְּעוּדָה בְּיִשְׂרָאֵל:

4:7   (Now this was the procedure formerly in Israel concerning the right of redemption and concerning the process of exchange; to confirm any matter, a man took off his sandal and gave it to his counterpart. This was the process of contract certification in Israel.)

וְזֹאת	dem pron, prox, f, s זֹאת (m, s זֶה) w/ וְ disj "Now this" According to *IBHS* §39.2.3c, a disjunctive *wāw* may introduce a parenthetical clause or sentence, and according to *BHRG* §40.8.2 (v), the *wāw* joins "clauses in which the content of the clause with וְ refers to *background information* necessary for understanding the other one better"; they translate the *wāw* "now."
לְפָנִים	n, m, pl, abs פָּנֶה√ פנה functioning as temp adv "formerly"
בְּיִשְׂרָאֵל	GN w/ בְּ "in Israel"
עַל־הַגְּאוּלָּה	n, f, s, abs גְּאוּלָּה√ גאל w/ def art and prep עַל√ עלה "concerning the right of redemption"
וְעַל־הַתְּמוּרָה	n, f, s, abs תְּמוּרָה√ מור w/ def art and prep עַל√ עלה and וְ conj "and concerning exchange, recompense"

לְקַיֵּם   v, D, inf, cs √קום w/ prep לְ "to establish, confirm, ratify"
According to Joüon §80h, "In the intensive conjugation, one has consonantal ו in עוֵּד *to embrace* Ps 119:61; elsewhere, one has י in place of ו as in Aramaic. The examples, rather rare and late, seem borrowed from Aramaic: קַיֵּם *to establish, to stand* (Aram. קַיֵּם) Esth 9:21 etc., Ruth 4:7; Ps 119:28, 106."

כָּל־דָּבָר   n, m, s, abs דָּבָר √דבר w/ n, m, s, cs כֹּל √כלל "every word, any matter"
Wms §105: "The substantive כֹּל followed by an indefinite substantive may have a distributive sense" (so also Brock §78).

שָׁלַף   v, G, pf, 3, m, s √שלף "he drew off, took off, removed"
Berg 2 §9l: "Occasionally, especially in poetry, a simple perfect before a perfect consecutive appears to have the significance of the perfect consecutive," here, "he would remove" (and understanding וְנָתַן as a perfect consecutive, i.e, "and he would give"). Though he cites our verse as an example, this does not seem necessary here, as my translation makes clear.

אִישׁ   n, m, s, abs אִישׁ √אנש? "a man"

נַעֲלוֹ   n, m, s, *st. pr.* נַעַל √נעל w/ 3, m, s, gen sx "his sandal"

וְנָתַן   v, G, pf, 3, m, s √נתן w/ ו conj "and he gave"
GKC §112h understands this as a perfect consecutive, as does Berg 2 §9l.

לְרֵעֵהוּ   n, m, s, *st. pr.* רֵעַ √רעה w/ 3, m, s, gen sx and prep לְ "to his neighbor"

וְזֹאת   dem pron, prox, f, s זֹאת (m, s זֶה) w/ ו conj "and this"

הַתְּעוּדָה   n, f, s, abs תְּעוּדָה √עוד w/ def art "the process of attestation, ratification"

בְּיִשְׂרָאֵל   GN w/ בְּ "in Israel"

4:8 וַיֹּאמֶר הַגֹּאֵל לְבֹעַז קְנֵה־לָךְ וַיִּשְׁלֹף נַעֲלוֹ׃

4:8   The kinsman-redeemer said to Boaz, "You buy it," and he took off his sandal.

וַיֹּאמֶר   v, G, impf, indic, 3, m, s √אמר w/ ו cons "and he said"

הַגֹּאֵל   v, G, act, ptc, m, s √גאל w/ def art "the redeemer"

לְבֹעַז   PN w/ prep לְ "to Boaz"

קְנֵה־לָךְ   v, G, impf, impv, 2, m, s √קנה w/ prep לְ w/ 2, m, s, gen sx "you redeem"

וַיִּשְׁלֹף   v, G, impf, indic, 3, m, s √שלף w/ ו cons "and he removed"

נַעֲלוֹ   n, m, s, *st. pr.* נַעַל √נעל w/ 3, m, s, gen sx "his sandal"

4:9 וַיֹּ֨אמֶר בֹּ֜עַז לַזְּקֵנִ֗ים וְכָל־הָעָם֙ עֵדִ֣ים אַתֶּ֣ם הַיּ֔וֹם כִּ֤י קָנִ֙יתִי֙ אֶת־כָּל־אֲשֶׁ֣ר לֶאֱלִימֶ֔לֶךְ וְאֵ֣ת כָּל־אֲשֶׁ֔ר לְכִלְי֖וֹן וּמַחְל֑וֹן מִיַּ֖ד נָעֳמִֽי׃

4:9   Boaz said to the elders and all the people, "You are witnesses today that I hereby buy all that belonged to Elimelech and all that belonged to Chilion and Mahlon from the hand of Naomi."

וַיֹּ֨אמֶר	v, G, impf, indic, 3, m, s √אמר אמר w/ ו cons "and he said"
בֹּ֜עַז	PN "Boaz"
לַזְּקֵנִ֗ים	adj, m, pl, abs זָקֵן √זקן w/ def art and prep לְ "to the elders"
וְכָל־הָעָם֙	n, m, s, abs עַם √עממ w/ def art and n, m, s, cs כֹּל √כלל and ו conj "and all of the people"
עֵדִ֣ים	n, m, pl, abs עֵד √עדה "witnesses"
אַתֶּ֣ם	indep pers pron, 2, m, s אַתֶּם √אנת "you"
הַיּ֔וֹם	n, m, s, abs יוֹם w/ def art "today"
כִּ֤י	conj כִּי "that, for, when"
קָנִ֙יתִי֙	v, G, pf, 1, c, s √קנה "I hereby buy" *IBHS* §30.5.1d: "An *instantaneous perfective* represents a situation occurring at the very instant the expression is being uttered.... I *acquire* (here and now)"; so also Joüon §112f: "*I acquire* (*here and now*, by my speaking)." Vance §10.4: "Sometimes a first-person perfective signifies that an event is commencing or occurring as the speaker is declaring it. This can be reflected in translation by a construction involving the word *hereby* and the use of the English present tense. This is called a *declarative* or, in some cases, a *performative perfective*."
אֶת־כָּל־	n, m, s, cs כֹּל √כלל w/ sign def dir obj "all that"
אֲשֶׁ֣ר	rel pron אֲשֶׁר √אשר "that"
לֶאֱלִימֶ֔לֶךְ	PN w/ prep לְ "belonged to Elimelech"
וְאֵ֣ת כָּל־אֲשֶׁ֔ר	rel pron אֲשֶׁר √אשר w/ n, m, s, cs כֹּל √כלל and sign def dir obj and ו conj "and all that"
לְכִלְי֖וֹן	PN w/ prep לְ "belonged to Chilion"
וּמַחְל֑וֹן	PN w/ ו conj "and Mahlon"

מִיַּד	n, f, s, cs יָד w/ prep מִן "from the hand of"
נָעֳמִי	PN "Naomi"

וְגַם אֶת־רוּת הַמֹּאֲבִיָּה֩ אֵ֨שֶׁת מַחְלוֹן֩ קָנִ֨יתִי לִ֜י לְאִשָּׁ֗ה לְהָקִ֤ים שֵׁם־הַמֵּת֙ עַל־ 4:10
נַחֲלָת֔וֹ וְלֹא־יִכָּרֵ֧ת שֵׁם־הַמֵּ֛ת מֵעִ֥ם אֶחָ֖יו וּמִשַּׁ֣עַר מְקוֹמ֑וֹ עֵדִ֥ים אַתֶּ֖ם הַיּֽוֹם׃

4:10   "And also Ruth, the Moabitess, the wife of Mahlon, I hereby buy for myself as a wife in order to raise up the name of the deceased over his estate and in order that the name of the deceased will not be cut off from among his relatives and from the gate of his place. You are witnesses today."

וְגַם	adv גַּם √גמם w/ ו conj "and also"
אֶת־רוּת	PN w/ sign def dir obj "Ruth"
הַמֹּאֲבִיָּה	gent adj, f, s, abs מוֹאֲבִי (m, s מוֹאָבִי) w/ def art "the Moabitess"
אֵשֶׁת	n, f, s, cs אִשָּׁה √אנשׁ "the wife of"
מַחְלוֹן	PN "Mahlon"
קָנִיתִי	v, G, pf, 1, c, s √קנה "I hereby buy"
לִי	prep לְ w/ 1, c, s, gen sx "for myself"
לְאִשָּׁה	n, m, s, abs אִשָּׁה √אנשׁ w/ prep לְ "for a wife"
לְהָקִים	v, H, inf, cs √קום w/ prep לְ "to raise up"
שֵׁם־הַמֵּת	v, G, act, ptc, m, s, abs √מות w/ def art and n, m, s, cs שֵׁם "the name of the deceased"
עַל־נַחֲלָתוֹ	n, f, s, *st. pr.* נַחֲלָה √נחל w/ 3, m, s, gen sx and prep עַל √עלה "over his estate"
וְלֹא־יִכָּרֵת	v, N, impf, indic, 3, m, s √כרת w/ neg part לֹא and ו conj "so that it may not be cut off"
שֵׁם־הַמֵּת	v, G, act, ptc, m, s, abs √מות w/ def art and n, m, s, cs שֵׁם "the name of the deceased"
מֵעִם	prep עִם √עמם w/ prep מִן "from among"
אֶחָיו	n, m, pl, *st. pr.* אָח √אחה w/ 3, m, s, gen sx "his brothers, relatives"
וּמִשַּׁעַר	n, m, s, cs שַׁעַר √שׁער w/ prep מִן and ו conj "and from the gate of"

מְקוֹמוֹ	n, m, s, *st. pr.* מָקוֹם √קום w/ 3, m, s, gen sx "his place"
עֵדִים	n, m, pl, abs עֵד √עדה "witnesses"
אַתֶּם	indep pers pron, 2, m, s אַתֶּם √אנת "you"
הַיּוֹם	n, m, s, abs יוֹם w/ def art "today"

4:11 וַיֹּאמְרוּ כָּל־הָעָם אֲשֶׁר־בַּשַּׁעַר וְהַזְּקֵנִים עֵדִים יִתֵּן יְהוָה אֶת־הָאִשָּׁה הַבָּאָה אֶל־בֵּיתֶךָ כְּרָחֵל ׀ וּכְלֵאָה אֲשֶׁר בָּנוּ שְׁתֵּיהֶם אֶת־בֵּית יִשְׂרָאֵל וַעֲשֵׂה־חַיִל בְּאֶפְרָתָה וּקְרָא־שֵׁם בְּבֵית לָחֶם׃

4:11   So all the people who were in the gate and the elders said, "We are witnesses. May YHWH grant that the wife who comes into your house be like Rachel and like Leah, who, between the two of them, built the house of Israel, so that you produce wealth in Ephrathah and so that you acquire fame in Bethlehem."

וַיֹּאמְרוּ	v, G, impf, indic, 3, m, pl √אמר w/ ו cons "and they said"
כָּל־הָעָם	n, m, s, abs עַם √עמם w/ def art and n, m, s, cs כֹּל √כלל "all the people"
אֲשֶׁר־בַּשַּׁעַר	n, m, s, abs שַׁעַר √שער w/ def art and prep בְּ and rel pron אֲשֶׁר √אשר "who were in the gate"
וְהַזְּקֵנִים	adj, m, pl, abs זָקֵן √זקן w/ def art and ו conj "and the elders"
עֵדִים	n, m, pl, abs עֵד √עדה "witnesses"
יִתֵּן	v, G, impf, juss, 3, m, s √נתן "may he give" On the jussive as blessing, see Berg 2 §10b.
יְהוָה	DN "YHWH"
אֶת־הָאִשָּׁה	n, f, s, abs אִשָּׁה √אנש w/ def art and sign def dir obj "the wife"
הַבָּאָה	v, G, act, ptc, f, s, abs √בוא w/ def art "who comes" Joüon §145e translates this "who is about to come."
אֶל־בֵּיתֶךָ	n, m, s, *st. pr.* בַּיִת w/ 2, m, s, gen sx and prep אֶל "to your house"
כְּרָחֵל	PN w/ prep כְּ "like Rachel"
וּכְלֵאָה	PN w/ prep כְּ and ו conj "and like Leah"
אֲשֶׁר	rel pron אֲשֶׁר √אשר "who"

בָּנוּ   v, G, pf, 3, c, pl √בנה "they built"

שְׁתֵּיהֶם   card, f, du, *st. pr.* שְׁנַיִם√שׁנהIII w/ 3, m, pl, gen sx "the two of them"
We have previously noted the gender agreement anomolies in Ruth. BL §79c simply states that הֶם is used for הֶן here.

אֶת־בֵּית   n, m, s, cs בַּיִת w/ sign def dir obj "the house of"

יִשְׂרָאֵל   PN "Israel"

וַעֲשֵׂה־   v, G, impf, impv, 2, m, s √עשה w/ ו conj "so that you may produce"
GKC §110i: "The imperative, when depending (with *wāw copulative*) upon a jussive (cohortative), or an interrogative sentence, frequently expresses also a consequence which is to be expected with certainty, and often a consequence which is intended, or in fact an intention." On a volitive after a jussive indicating a result or purpose clause, see Seow, p. 244.

חַיִל   n, m, s, abs חַיִל√חיל "wealth"

בְּאֶפְרָתָה   GN w/ prep בְּ "in Ephrathah"

וּקְרָא־שֵׁם   n, m, s, abs שֵׁם and v, G, impf, impv, 2, m, s √קרא w/ ו conj "and so that you may call a name," i.e., "so that you may be famous"

בְּבֵית לָחֶם   GN w/ prep בְּ "in Bethlehem"

4:12 וִיהִי בֵיתְךָ כְּבֵית פֶּרֶץ אֲשֶׁר־יָלְדָה תָמָר לִיהוּדָה מִן־הַזֶּרַע אֲשֶׁר יִתֵּן יְהוָה לְךָ מִן־הַנַּעֲרָה הַזֹּאת:

4:12 "And may your house be like the house of Perez, whom Tamar bore to Judah, from the seed that YHWH will give to you from this young woman."

וִיהִי   v, G, impf, juss, 3, m, s √היה w/ ו conj "and may it be"

בֵיתְךָ   n, m, s, *st. pr.* בַּיִת w/ 2, m, s, gen sx "your house"

כְּבֵית   n, m, s, cs בַּיִת w/ prep כְּ "like the house of"

פֶּרֶץ   PN "Perez"

אֲשֶׁר־יָלְדָה   v, G, pf, 3, f, s √ילד w/ rel pron אֲשֶׁר√אשר "whom [Tamar] bore"

תָמָר   PN "Tamar"

לִיהוּדָה   PN w/ prep לְ "to Judah"

מִן־הַזֶּרַע	n, m, s, abs זֶרַע√זרע w/ def art and prep מִן "from the seed"
אֲשֶׁר	rel pron אֲשֶׁר√אשר "that"
יִתֵּן	v, G, impf, indic, 3, m, s √נתן "he will give"
יְהוָה	DN "YHWH"
לְךָ	prep לְ w/ 2, m, s, gen sx "to you"
מִן־הַנַּעֲרָה	n, f, s, abs נַעֲרָה√נער w/ def art and prep מִן "from the young woman"
הַזֹּאת	dem adj, prox, f, s זֹאת (m, s זֶה) w/ def art "this"

4:13 וַיִּקַּח בֹּעַז אֶת־רוּת וַתְּהִי־לוֹ לְאִשָּׁה וַיָּבֹא אֵלֶיהָ וַיִּתֵּן יְהוָה לָהּ הֵרָיוֹן וַתֵּלֶד בֵּן:

4:13 Boaz took Ruth, and she became his wife. He went in to her, and YHWH gave conception to her, and she bore a son.

וַיִּקַּח	v, G, impf, indic, 3, m, s לקח√ w/ ו cons "and he took"
בֹּעַז	PN "Boaz"
אֶת־רוּת	PN w/ sign def dir obj "Ruth"
וַתְּהִי־לוֹ	v, G, impf, indic, 3, f, s היה√ w/ prep לְ w/ 3, m, s, gen sx and ו cons "and she was to him"
לְאִשָּׁה	n, f, s, abs אִשָּׁה√אנש w/ prep לְ "for a wife"
וַיָּבֹא	v, G, impf, indic, 3, m, s בוא√ w/ ו cons "and he came"
אֵלֶיהָ	prep אֶל w/ 3, f, s, gen sx "to her"
וַיִּתֵּן	v, G, impf, indic, 3, m, s נתן√ w/ ו cons "and he gave"
יְהוָה	DN "YHWH"
לָהּ	prep לְ w/ 3, f, s, gen sx "to her"
הֵרָיוֹן	n, m, s, abs הֵרָיוֹן√הרה "conception, pregnancy" On וֹן- as an abstract noun–forming suffix, see Joüon §88b and and BL §61cq.
וַתֵּלֶד	v, G, impf, indic, 3, f, s ילד√ w/ ו cons "and she bore"
בֵּן	n, m, s, abs בֵּן√בנה? "son"

4:14 וַתֹּאמַ֤רְנָה הַנָּשִׁים֙ אֶֽל־נָעֳמִ֔י בָּר֣וּךְ יְהוָ֔ה אֲשֶׁ֠ר לֹ֣א הִשְׁבִּ֥ית לָ֛ךְ גֹּאֵ֖ל הַיּ֑וֹם וְיִקָּרֵ֥א שְׁמ֖וֹ בְּיִשְׂרָאֵֽל׃

4:14   The women said to Naomi, "Blessed be YHWH, who did not put an end to a kinsman-redeemer for you today. May he become famous in Israel."

וַתֹּאמַ֤רְנָה	v, G, impf, indic, 3, f, pl √אמר w/ ו cons "and they said"
הַנָּשִׁים֙	n, f, pl, abs אִשָּׁה √אנש w/ def art "the women"
אֶֽל־נָעֳמִ֔י	PN w/ prep אֶל "to Naomi"
בָּר֣וּךְ	v, G, pass, ptc, m, s, abs √ברך "blessed"
יְהוָ֔ה	DN "YHWH"
אֲשֶׁ֠ר	rel pron אֲשֶׁר √אשר "who"
לֹ֣א הִשְׁבִּ֥ית	v, H, pf, 3, m, s √שבת w/ neg part לֹא "he did not cause to cease"
לָ֛ךְ	prep לְ w/ 2, f, s, gen sx "to you"
גֹּאֵ֖ל	v, G, act, ptc, m, s √גאל "a redeemer"
הַיּ֑וֹם	n, m, s, abs יוֹם w/ def art "today"
וְיִקָּרֵ֥א	v, N, impf, indic, 3, m, s √קרא w/ ו conj "and may it be called"
שְׁמ֖וֹ	n, m, s, *st. pr.* שֵׁם w/ 3, m, s, gen sx "his name"
בְּיִשְׂרָאֵֽל	GN w/ prep בְּ "in Israel"

4:15 וְהָ֤יָה לָךְ֙ לְמֵשִׁ֣יב נֶ֔פֶשׁ וּלְכַלְכֵּ֖ל אֶת־שֵׂיבָתֵ֑ךְ כִּ֣י כַלָּתֵ֤ךְ אֲֽשֶׁר־אֲהֵבַ֙תֶךְ֙ יְלָדַ֔תּוּ אֲשֶׁר־הִיא֙ ט֣וֹבָה לָ֔ךְ מִשִּׁבְעָ֖ה בָּנִֽים׃

4:15   "May he be a restorer of life to you to sustain your grey head; for your daughter-in-law, who has loved you, has born him; she is better to you than seven sons."

וְהָ֤יָה	v, G, pf, 3, m, s √היה w/ ו cons "and may he be to you"
לָ֖ךְ	prep לְ w/ 2, f, s, gen sx "to you"
לְמֵשִׁ֣יב	v, H, ptc, m, s, cs √שוב w/ prep לְ "for a returner of"

According to Joüon §31c, one may expect the accent of a word that is accented on the final syllable to retard to the penultima (such as לְמֵשִׁיב) when the word is juxtaposed to a word with the accent on the first syllable (such as נֶפֶשׁ; see also תֹּאכַל לֶחֶם in Gen 1:5) but only if the last syllable is closed and has a short syllable. Since לְמֵשִׁיב has a *î* in the last syllable, the tone does not retard.

נֶפֶשׁ	n, f, s, abs נֶפֶשׁ √נפשׁ "soul"
וּלְכַלְכֵּל	v, D, inf, cs √כול w/ prep לְ w/ וֹ conj "and to sustain" On this form, see Berg 2 §20c.
אֶת־שֵׂיבָתֵךְ	n, f, s, *st. pr.* שֵׂיבָה √שׁיב w/ 2, f, s, gen sx and sign def dir obj "your grey head"
כִּי	conj כִּי "for, because, that"
כַּלָּתֵךְ	n, f, s, *st. pr.* כַּלָּה √כלל w/ 2, f, s, gen sx "your daughter-in-law"
אֲשֶׁר־	rel pron אֲשֶׁר √אשׁר "who"
אֲהֵבָתֶךְ	v, G, pf, 3, f, s √אהב w/ 2, f, s, acc sx "she has loved you" On the form of this perfect verb with an accusative suffix, see GKC §59g and Berg 2 §4f, who reads with most MSS a *qāmeṣ* under the *bêt* instead of the *pataḥ*.
יְלָדַתּוּ	v, G, pf, 3, f, s √ילד w/ 3, m, s, acc sx "she has born him"
אֲשֶׁר־הִיא	indep pers pron, 3, f, s הִיא w/ rel pron אֲשֶׁר √אשׁר "who is" The pronoun is resumptive, picking up the subject—Ruth—again, which is necessary after the intervening יְלָדַתּוּ with its third masculine singular suffix, which might be confused as the antecedent of this אֲשֶׁר. So similarly Brock §152a. According to Joüon §158g, "the retrospective (i.e., resumptive) subject pronoun, in nominal clauses, is usually with an adjective or a participle." See also Driver, p. 271.
טוֹבָה	adj, f, s, abs טוֹב √טוב "good; better"
לָךְ	prep לְ w/ 2, f, s, gen sx "to you"
מִשִּׁבְעָה	card, f, s, abs שֶׁבַע √שׁבע w/ prep מִן "than seven"
בָּנִים	n, m, pl, abs בֵּן √בנה? "sons"

4:16 וַתִּקַּח נָעֳמִי אֶת־הַיֶּ֫לֶד וַתְּשִׁתֵ֫הוּ בְחֵיקָהּ וַתְּהִי־לוֹ לְאֹמֶֽנֶת׃

4:16   Then Naomi took the child, placed him on her lap, and became his nurse.

וַתִּקַּח	v, G, impf, indic, 3, f, s √לקח w/ ו cons "and she took"
נָעֳמִי	PN "Naomi"
אֶת־הַיֶּ֫לֶד	n, m, s, abs יֶ֫לֶד √ילד w/ def art and sign def dir obj "the child"
וַתְּשִׁתֵ֫הוּ	v, G, impf, indic, 3, f, s √שׁית w/ 3, m, s, acc sx and ו cons "and she placed him"
בְחֵיקָהּ	n, m, s, *st. pr.* חֵיק √חוק w/ 3, f, s, gen sx and prep בְּ "on her lap"
וַתְּהִי־לוֹ	v, G, impf, indic, 3, f, s √היה w/ prep לְ w/ 3, m, s, gen sx and ו cons "and she became for him"
לְאֹמֶֽנֶת	v, G, act, ptc, f, s, abs √אמן w/ prep לְ "as a nurse"

4:17 וַתִּקְרֶ֫אנָה לוֹ הַשְּׁכֵנוֹת שֵׁם לֵאמֹר יֻלַּד־בֵּן לְנָעֳמִי וַתִּקְרֶ֫אנָה שְׁמוֹ עוֹבֵד הוּא אֲבִי־יִשַׁי אֲבִי דָוִד׃

4:17   The neighborhood women gave him a name, saying, "A son has been born to Naomi!" They named him Obed. He was the father of Jesse, the father of David.

וַתִּקְרֶ֫אנָה לוֹ	v, G, impf, indic, 3, f, pl √קרא w/ prep לְ w/ 3, m, s, gen sx and ו cons "and they called him"
הַשְּׁכֵנוֹת	adj, f, pl, abs שָׁכֵן √שׁכן w/ def art "the neighborhood women"
שֵׁם	n, m, s, abs שֵׁם "a name"
לֵאמֹר	v, G, inf, cs √אמר w/ prep לְ "saying"
יֻלַּד־בֵּן	v, Dp, pf, 3, m, s √ילד w/ n, m, s, abs בֵּן "a son has been born"
לְנָעֳמִי	PN w/ prep לְ "to Naomi"
וַתִּקְרֶ֫אנָה	v, G, impf, indic, 3, f, pl √קרא w/ ו cons "and they called"
שְׁמוֹ	n, m, s, *st. pr.* שֵׁם w/ 3, m, s, gen sx "his name"
עוֹבֵד	v, G, act, ptc, m, s, abs √עבד "server" PN "Obed"

הוּא	indep pers pron, 3, m, s הוּא "he"
אֲבִי־יִשַׁי	PN w/ n, m, s, cs אָב √אבה "the father of Jesse"
	If this name were transliterated strictly, it would be *Yīšay*
אֲבִי דָוִד	PN w/ n, m, s, cs אָב √אבה "the father of David"

4:18 וְאֵ֙לֶּה֙ תּוֹלְד֣וֹת פֶּ֔רֶץ פֶּ֖רֶץ הוֹלִ֥יד אֶת־חֶצְרֽוֹן׃

4:18 Now these are the generations of Perez: Perez fathered Hezron;

וְאֵ֙לֶּה֙	dem pron, prox, f, pl אֵלֶּה w/ וּ disj "now these"
	IBHS §39.2.3c: "A disjunctive-*waw* clause may also shift the scene or refer to new participants; the disjunction may come at the beginning or end of a larger episode or it may 'interrupt' one.... [A]t the conclusion, further developments are briefly sketched or the narrated episode is put in context." Translations of Ruth 4:6–8 and 4:18, 21–22 are given as examples.
תּוֹלְדוֹת	n, f, pl, cs תּוֹלֵדָה √ילד "the generations of"
פֶּרֶץ	PN "Perez"
פֶּרֶץ	PN "Perez"
הוֹלִיד	v, H, pf, 3, m, s √ילד "he fathered"
אֶת־חֶצְרוֹן	PN w/ sign def dir obj "Hezron"

4:19 וְחֶצְרוֹן֙ הוֹלִ֣יד אֶת־רָ֔ם וְרָ֖ם הוֹלִ֥יד אֶת־עַמִּֽינָדָֽב׃

4:19 Hezron fathered Ram; Ram fathered Amminadab;

וְחֶצְרוֹן֙	PN w/ וּ conj "Hezron"
הוֹלִיד	v, H, pf, 3, m, s √ילד "he fathered"
אֶת־רָם	PN w/ sign def dir obj "Ram"
וְרָם	PN w/ וּ conj "and Ram"
הוֹלִיד	v, H, pf, 3, m, s √ילד "he fathered"
אֶת־עַמִּֽינָדָֽב	PN w/ sign def dir obj "Amminadab"

4:20 וְעַמִּינָדָב֙ הוֹלִ֣יד אֶת־נַחְשׁ֔וֹן וְנַחְשׁ֖וֹן הוֹלִ֥יד אֶת־שַׂלְמָֽה׃

4:20   Amminadab fathered Nahshon; Nahshon fathered Salmon;

וְעַמִּינָדָב֙	PN "Amminadab"
הוֹלִיד	v, H, pf, 3, m, s √ילד "he fathered"
אֶת־נַחְשׁוֹן	PN w/ sign def dir obj "Nahshon"
וְנַחְשׁוֹן	PN w/ ו conj "and Nahshon"
הוֹלִיד	v, H, pf, 3, m, s √ילד "he fathered"
אֶת־שַׂלְמָה	PN w/ sign def dir obj "Salmon"

4:21 וְשַׂלְמוֹן֙ הוֹלִ֣יד אֶת־בֹּ֔עַז וּבֹ֖עַז הוֹלִ֥יד אֶת־עוֹבֵֽד׃

4:21   Salmon fathered Boaz; Boaz fathered Obed;

וְשַׂלְמוֹן֙	PN w/ ו conj "and Salmon"
הוֹלִיד	v, H, pf, 3, m, s √ילד "he fathered"
אֶת־בֹּעַז	PN w/ sign def dir obj "Boaz"
וּבֹעַז	PN w/ ו conj "and Boaz"
הוֹלִיד	v, H, pf, 3, m, s √ילד "he fathered"
אֶת־עוֹבֵד	PN w/ sign def dir obj "Obed"

4:22 וְעֹבֵד֙ הוֹלִ֣יד אֶת־יִשָׁ֔י וְיִשַׁ֖י הוֹלִ֥יד אֶת־דָּוִֽד׃

4:22   Obed fathered Jesse; and Jesse fathered David.

וְעֹבֵד֙	PN w/ ו conj "and Obed"
הוֹלִיד	v, H, pf, 3, m, s √ילד "he fathered"
אֶת־יִשָׁי	PN w/ sign def dir obj "Jesse"
וְיִשַׁי	PN w/ ו conj "and Jesse"
הוֹלִיד	v, H, pf, 3, m, s √ילד "he fathered"
אֶת־דָּוִד	PN w/ sign def dir obj "David"